Conjuring as a Craft

Conjuring as a Craft

IAN ADAIR

Illustrations by the author, whose hands
appear in the action photographs
taken by
A. C. Littlejohns, AMPA and
John Willis

South Brunswick and New York:
A. S. Barnes and Co.

Library of Congress Catalogue Card Number: 70-140323

A. S. Barnes and Co., Inc.
Cranbury, New Jersey 08512

ISBN 0-498-07854-X
Printed in Great Britain

to EDWIN

Contents

List of Illustrations

1

Introduction to Magic

SINCE the beginning magic has fascinated and amazed people all over the world. In Biblical times conjuring played an important part in the religion and the entertainment of the masses. In the 'Golden Age of Magic'—1910 to 1930—magicians topped the bills at every major music-hall in the world. During the war years magic played an important part in the entertainment of the troops and, with the cessation of hostilities and the commencement of television, conjuring really came into its own, for here, and on stage and in cabaret, the person who could *bewilder* his audience, capping this by *entertaining* them as well, was presenting double value for money.

Socially, too, the man who could present a few minor miracles with items picked up at random in the home, at the bar, or in the office, was the lion of the evening, remembered, talked about, and admired.

Most people enter the magical world of make-believe as young children when a conjurer has been engaged to entertain in the home, at a concert, at a factory party. The child's world of fantasy and 'let's pretend' assumes a new

11

dimension in this new delightful world where the impossible becomes possible. Often this interest is furthered by a 'box of tricks' or a book on conjuring.

On television, viewers who cannot normally attend live shows in the metropolis are able to see the 'greats' of magic in action—as it were right in their own homes. The magic of television is explicable to science, but the magic which the conjurer presents is inexplicable. The magician receives credit for his skill, adroitness, personality, and showmanship.

Let us make our picture complete by emphasising that a person's interest in conjuring (*your* interest, for you have bought this book) is not an inference that he wishes himself to become a professional magician touring round the various clubs, theatres or television studios. That indeed would be rather a bold attitude to adopt at this early stage. Assuming the reader is interested in the basic principles used in conjuring and their use to present entertainment, 'magic' as we call it is a tremendously enjoyable, relaxing pastime or hobby; one which brings real pleasure and interest; one which can help your social status; one which can help you overcome inhibitions and complexes. Magic is a hobby which *will help you to develop your personality* and to become more successful in your general life.

If, later on, the student wishes to delve deeper into the aspects of the art, he can and *will* find that to be able to entertain can pay handsomely. Magic can become a very lucrative business indeed, providing a steady source of extra income or becoming a full time and highly paid profession.

Having been in magic for some twenty years it is of never failing interest to me to note the types and classes of people who are drawn in to become devotees, deriving pleasure from our art. We have doctors, dustmen, solicitors, undertakers, plumbers, vicars, executive businessmen, right up to royalty. His Highness the Duke of Edinburgh is a member of the Magic Circle, one of the most important magical organisations (together with the International Brotherhood of Magicians) in this country. He has attended some of the Magic Circle meetings, learning the basic principles of the art. There is often a magician present to entertain at one of the royal events, whether it is a party for the royal children or at a dinner.

Magic is an *art*. It is an art that requires practice but it is one that can be learnt.

Teach six people how to do a simple trick then watch the results as they perform it. Five may be able to do the trick correctly and well but only one person will have bothered to *present* it properly. This sixth person will have given the performance of the item some thought and will inject into its presentation something of his own personality. Maybe he will not realise this at the time but his audience will. He is the man who can not only 'do the trick', but can also present it in a slick and entertaining manner. His patter and actions 'raise the trick up', he handles his props in a deft manner, one phase of the trick blends naturally into the other with smooth continuity. The audience do not have to be told of these things, they are only conscious that *this* man is an artiste.

The same rules which apply to the presentation of a trick apply to many things in life. A person may well be able to afford a most expensive violin but this doesn't mean that he can play it; his efforts may well be discordant. Yet give an old timer, an artiste, a cheaper model and he can play melodies—beautiful music which his audience could listen to all evening.

With the written word the same applies.

A piece of poetry can be delivered with sincerity and feeling, it can make us feel good, happy, or sad, de-

13

pending on the words of the author and the rendering of the performer. Alas, too often, the composer's beautiful words are turned into a dirge, a bore, by the lack of sympathetic feeling and histrionic ability of the latter.

There is a right and a wrong way to do everything in the world. If the reader wishes truly to entertain his or her friends these first paragraphs will mean as much as the tricks which follow in this publication.

I have often been sadly amused when someone who has learned the secret of a certain trick immediately exclaims 'I can do it!' CAN HE? Nine times out of ten he would be the first person to admit that he just could not stand up and face *any* audience, let alone present an entertaining interlude of tricks which could be the talk of the evening. So what *is* magic? Magic is an art developed over centuries and handed down to us from enthusiastic people who have enjoyed the evolution of conjuring tricks into seemingly impossible miracles. As time moves, so does magic. There is always something new and different to learn and to see.

My work has brought me into contact with over 10,000 magicians throughout the world and this is only a very small percentage of the enthusiasts who owe a lot to magic and to whom magic owes so much. What can magic do *for you*? That is a good question and one which can be answered in different ways.

I have already mentioned that one doesn't have to be a *touring professional* to be in magic and there is a whole army of semi-professional and amateur magicians all over the world. Name any country and it has its own magicians. Colour or creed doesn't matter, rich or poor is immaterial. Magicians assemble in brotherly fraternity to discuss, to practise and to elevate their art.

Magic can be presented under any conditions. In the

social life it is a boon—at home, for instance, whilst entertaining friends to dinner a short interlude of conjuring
after the meal can certainly make an evening worth talking
about (maybe even excuse your wife's cooking!).

At 'the local', in the club, at the bar, a few tricks with
a pack of cards, or easily available bits—matches, bottle tops
and so on—can always be counted on to make the 'boys'
talk. It can gain the performer much credit, making him the
centre of attraction. At Church and charitable concerts the
man who maybe cannot sing, dance, or tell funny stories,
can turn his hand to entertaining his audience with magical
effects, immediately becoming the star of the evening. How
many times have people afterwards said 'I never realised
that Mr - - - was so clever'.

Many of the television and sponsored competition talent-
shows include a magician on the bill; he is a speciality act,
the touch of variety that is the spice of life. There are so
many would-be singers but the magician is far more of a
novelty; many have stopped the show, gaining the highest
awards, cash prizes, paid-for holidays at holiday camps, and
similar rewards.

Theatres, nightclubs, and television programmes, are
always looking for new personalities, whether they be
singers, comedians, dancers, jugglers, or magicians. Magic
is a wonderful vehicle for displaying your personality. As
you skilfully present your magical problems you are able to
inject into the performance a great deal of your own indi-
viduality. If your personality is a likeable one you may
well have your chance of becoming a star. Personality is
so important.

Think of the magicians, and the odds are you will think
of those who have appeared on your television screens in
all parts of the world. Maybe you will be able to think of
just a few, not because there is any shortage of magical

talent, but rather that these are the few who on the strength of their *personality* have won the acclaim of audiences and thus the confidence of television producers.

In Great Britain we think of David Nixon, who has such a charming personality; while in the USA Dia Vernon is named as one of the top rank professionals who adds charm to his magic. Dutch television viewers when asked to name a magician will instantly reply Fred Kapps; and in India the name of Sorcar, who has been acclaimed the world's greatest magician, is a household name on television and in the world of the theatre.

In nightclubs and working men's clubs (and in the North of England especially and in Wales there are many hundreds of these), magic, when entertainingly presented, is often on the programme. On stage, in variety, review, or pantomime, and after-dinner shows, school concerts, socials, and impromptu gatherings, magic is an acceptable diversion.

Probably it is at its best, bringing happiness to the audience and also to the performer, at children's parties in the home, at hospitals, institutions, and so on. A children's party these days would not seem complete without a magician. He is accepted as being the perfect entertainer at such a function, for his show brings with it audience participation, action, and fun. After the food and the games comes the 'magical highspot', often talked about for months afterwards by the children and by many remembered forever more.

Everyone is interested in making money, and money can be made from magic, even though one has another job of work to do during the daytime. In the evenings or at weekends large fees are to be obtained from the slick performance of magical entertainment. I know of some hundreds of performers who make more money from their engagements over the weekends, especially at busy periods

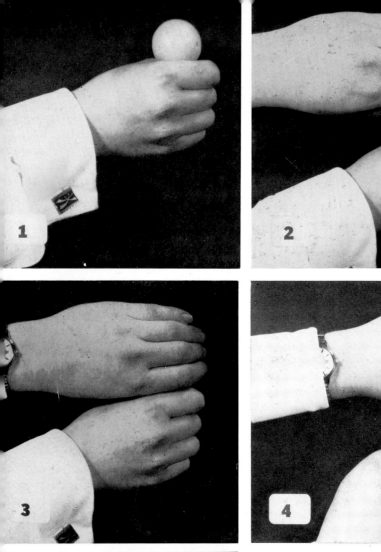

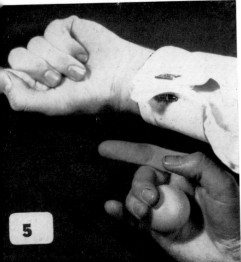

Page 18: Vanishing a billiard ball (1) *Ball rests on top of closed fist;* (2) *left hand comes forward;* (3) *left hand covers ball. Ball drops into right hand;* (4) *left hand moves away with supposed ball. Right hand points;* (5) *back view showing position before the 'vanish'*

over Christmas, than they do from their normal employment. Their employment acts as a buffer—the insurance for when the engagements are not so plentiful. Some plunge from semi-professionalism into the field of the professional entertainer. Of course, it doesn't always pay off. Sometimes the magician, although being first rate, is not a good business man; or it may well be that he is not accepted as a professional by the agents through whom he works.

What is the first essential you have to learn to become a magician? You have bought this book and you want to learn some tricks; you also want to know some of the magic secrets which have always interested you. That is a good start. You are interested in conjuring and you know the goals which your success in this sphere can lead to. What then are the next steps you must take?

Step number one, the essential you must face before embarking on this voyage of discovery, is that you must *practise.* You must study the routine and the secret of the trick, then you must practise its working and presentation *over and over again* until you can perform the trick almost blindfolded. There is no excuse for fumbling and fiddling around with an item; you are to blame if it goes wrong. You can't blame the trick. The tricks which I shall later describe have all been tried and tested; they have been presented before an audience and proved to be good, entertaining, and practical.

The fact that one performer doesn't get as much out of a trick as another doesn't mean that the trick is not a good one. It could be that the audience is unresponsive, for not all audiences are enthusiastic. He could be presenting the trick under poor conditions, with poor lighting perhaps, or with people looking over his shoulder. Maybe the performer doesn't feel too well or has an 'off' night, in which case it would have been better for him to stay at home! One should feel on top of the world and full of enthusiasm before running through the repertoire of mysteries.

An experienced magician recently said 'It's not how many tricks you can do but how many you can present really well'. In other words it is better knowing four tricks thoroughly, having practised them until they are perfect, than having learnt a hundred but giving none of them a proper performance. A concert pianist would never dream of giving a performance after only rehearsing the work a few times, for he would disgrace himself and let the composer of the composition down. So a magician should practise his tricks in front of a mirror, carefully watching not only for exposures but for unnecessary gestures and movements. He should rehearse his patter, cutting out repetitious statements, making it flow smoothly with the magic. Unfunny jokes or dull patter can make the trick an unappealing one, no matter how good or how bad the magic is.

So practice is the *first* essential of conjuring. Practise every item you wish to perform *over and over again*. If it is still not perfect, do not present the trick; put it to one side and try another one which you feel you can perform better. Later you may feel that you can go back and try the first problem again, and you may well find the snags which you first encountered have been overcome. Practice makes perfect and can turn a simple conjuring trick into a masterpiece of mystery.

The second rule of magic is *secrecy*. Without secrecy we would have no magic. Magic is bewildering, baffling, and, when presented correctly, entertaining. Leave your audience mystified and with an impression of your cleverness. When you show how a trick is done you do not gain any credit, but instead destroy the glamour which first surrounded it.

Most people are disappointed at knowing how simply they have been fooled. The magician's job is to fool his audience as well as to amuse and entertain them, which is what the public expect of him; furthermore, remember that the secrets of magic are not yours to expose. Magical methods have been built, one on the other, over centuries. Exposing magical secrets is so easy, but keeping these to oneself, remembering the numerous magicians who use these methods, is a far greater achievement. By doing this the conjurer brings credit to himself and to magic generally, and thus to his fellow magicians all over the world.

The same rules apply to a badly presented trick. At one time or other the reader must have seen a conjurer present a trick poorly, exposing the method. By doing this he has ruined not only his own reputation but that of others who follow and perform the same trick. Sometimes, of course, exposure can come through no fault of the performer, perhaps on television through a bad camera angle, preventing the particular trick being shown for years to come. Other magicians who wish to present the problem have to start at 'Square one', devising a new method or new presentation, for the secret of the original is no longer theirs but shared by millions. *Practice* is our first essential and *secrecy* is our second. They go together, for without either we can never satisfactorily present our magical effects.

One could argue that here, in your hands, is a book of secrets which is being distributed amongst laymen all over the world. Surely *this* must constitute an exposure. The answer is *No* it doesn't! This book is a volume of secrets which has come into the hands of someone who obviously is deeply interested in the art of magic. If a person is interested in cookery he will go out of his way to buy the best publications on the subject. The secrets of the master chefs have been written up, they are available to all who are sufficiently keen to seek them out. We all learn from each other and through the medium of a book we can discover tried and tested methods, but at the same time we can keep the secret to ourselves. That is why the book you have before you is so secret. If a friend, knowing that you have this book, wishes to read it, refuse to part with it; you have paid cash for it for your own pleasure and if your friend is so interested tell him to buy a copy for himself. If he does, then he too must be interested. By passing it over to him to glance quickly over the contents you are exposing your purchased secrets. *Keep the secrets of magic to yourself.*

What kind of tricks am I going to present, you may well ask. Now it is assumed that the reader does not, at this stage, wish to spend a tremendous amount of money on the special magical apparatus which is sold exclusively to magicians. The items used in this book are, for the most part, commonplace commodities which are easily available around the average home: matchboxes, paper clips, cards, coins, paper, etc. Because these are ordinary objects with which people are familiar your magic becomes more convincing. The tricks described can all be presented close up, with your audience around you, or, if you prefer, you can work on a platform before a seated audience.

Your props will cost so little and yet the effects which you achieve may be great. There is not necessarily any relationship between what an item costs and its impact on the audience. Chan Canasta, Al Koran, David Nixon, all present clever magic with small items, close up on the television screen, and a routine, well devised and performed, using these homely objects can gain more audience approval than one based on spending hundreds of pounds on elaborate cabinets from which to produce young ladies!

My tricks are suitable for anyone, from the beginner to

the more experienced magician. Where possible most have been given a twist—a sting in their tail—to add piquancy and zest to a more orthodox magical presentation.

Magic provides a never-ending source of wonder, with a legion of tricks. Articles can vanish, appear, reappear, change places, penetrate through solid matter, change colour, levitate, be suspended, and change into something completely different; and many variations are possible on this basic structure.

Many books would be needed just to list the tricks which have been invented and used by magicians. It is possible, and very probable, that after studying the tricks in these pages that you will come up with little moves and improvements of your own, that you will add your own personal variations and invent your own magic. Indeed you will then be presenting something which others have never seen. You will have your own material which does not appear in other books nor is it sold by magical dealers.

I have explained how the kind of tricks you use in your performance will depend upon the sort of person you are and the type of entertainment you wish to present. Maybe you will decide to perform close-up magic before friends, at the drop of a hat, and with normal everyday objects, dazzling the onlookers. A close-up show should always appear impromptu. Don't force your magic on to your guests, but wait to be asked to do a trick, or bring the trick logically into your conversation. For example, someone may be talking about money and you say. 'Talking about money I knew a chap, once, who could take a penny like this, pop it into his hand and it would vanish,' and so on. Thus you go into your magic in a smooth manner. Once you have presented your first close-up trick others can easily follow.

Do not give your audience too much at one time. Leave your audience wanting more, tell them there will always be another time. It is better to leave in this manner rather than to bore your friends with a succession of tricks.

In many cases, friends will ask, 'Oh, do that again. Let Mary see it, she missed it,' and so on. The temptation is there to repeat the effect but I strongly advise the student of magic not to repeat a trick. Perform something similar by all means, a trick which has a different ending maybe, thus the effect is fooling and entertaining to the person who first saw it as well as to the others. The surprise element would be missing if you were to repeat the effect exactly as you showed it at first; furthermore, onlookers are searching for the slight flaw in the effect which they may have missed the first time and thus your magic may be exposed. As your knowledge of magic grows you will be able to improvise quickly and to present many effects with simple items.

Many magical enthusiasts use conjuring to help them during their work and in their social activities. I know of many commercial representatives who go from town to town taking orders for the firms they work for. They are always welcome because they are always able to take a trick from their pocket and perform it. Their visits are looked forward to, they are remembered as personalities, and consequently their order-books are always full!

Of course, others prefer to present their magic for a seated audience, varying from professional variety and revues to Scout evenings at the Church Hall. Items chosen for the stage performance should be visual and, ideally, the act should last no longer than twelve to fifteen minutes. Try to keep your performance well balanced and varied.

There are a few rules to be followed for stage performances.

The beginner is advised not to overdo stage make-up; very little is actually required, in small shows, none at all.

INTRODUCTION TO MAGIC

The performer should appear well dressed at all times. His appearance is as important as his tricks. When he walks on the stage, all eyes are on him. Many a performer has been ruined by presenting a rough unkempt appearance. Make sure that your suit is immaculate in every way. Re-check until you are satisfied that you look like a gentleman and like a magician.

Your hands should be spotlessly clean, for they are watched throughout the entire show. When you stand on the stage you are putting yourself 'up to be shot at'.

Your apparatus should look smart and clean. Remember that you are supposed to be a magician so play the part of one.

Cabaret work differs from all other types of performing. When I say cabaret, I mean working on the dance-floor, the audience almost, or completely, surrounding you. Naturally, the tricks which you perform under these special conditions have to be carefully selected. Playing to an audience 'in front' may be easy but playing with the audience on all sides is another matter. One must move around, pattering to various parts of the audience yet always retaining control of the whole. Speak loudly and clearly so that everyone can hear you make quite sure that they all are fully aware of the magical effects which are taking place.

It is important to find out before your performance the conditions under which you will be working. You are then able to arrange your show correctly and ensure that your performance is a smooth and appropriate one.

Watch out when you are performing, especially in drawing-rooms, for decorative mirrors on walls. Work away from these. If you explain your difficulties to your booker he will probably remove the mirror. One performer I know always carries a large flag with him, magically producing this at the start, then fastening it with the aid of two small

25

rubber suckers over the offending mirror. He has performed his first effect and at the same time overcome what would be a real difficulty, a fact that the audience understands and appreciates.

Typists in an office can make mistakes which can be secretly altered and corrected but a magician is presenting his contribution on-stage 'live' in front of the audience. Still, with experience he will be able to overcome any mishaps which occur. Always keeping command of the situation. *Don't panic,* there is always a way out. Remember that the audience is not fully aware of the *effect* which you set out to accomplish, so you have a decided *advantage* in the event of any trick misfiring. Try to anticipate things which could go wrong during your show and think to yourself how you would react if this particular misfortune happened. Thus, in the event of a mishap you will be *prepared* and able to continue. You will gain a reputation for being a master of the 'ad lib', yet all these things can really be rehearsed. The important thing is to *know what you are doing* and to remember that you are there to entertain your audience.

I wish you good luck with your pursuance of our wonderful art of magic. I hope that one day we may meet face-to-face and I will be the first to say, 'Welcome to our Brotherhood of Magicians.' In exchange, I would be delighted to hear that your comment might perhaps be, 'Thank you for your book of magic which started me on the road to success'.

2

Tricks with Almost Anything

RED, WHITE AND BLUE

PATRIOTISM doesn't really enter into this effect, although it can come into the patter theme if you wish.

Three cards are shown and dropped into a hat. One is red, one is white, and one is blue.

The three cards are shown singly, the red and blue ones being removed.

What is the colour of the card that is left in the hat? Wrong!—the Magician shows that the hat is EMPTY!

The white card is produced from the pocket. How did it get there? 'It must have gone BY AIR,' says the conjurer as he turns the card over to show an AIR-MAIL label stuck on it!

HERE'S HOW

Three pieces of card are used, roughly about playing card size. One of these should be painted or crayoned (or coloured paper may be stuck on to one side) so that it shows white on one side and blue on the other. The second card, as illustrated, is feked. On one side half the card is coloured red, leaving a portion of white card to appear like a white card at an angle. Alternatively, colour the whole of the surface of the card red, then stick on a small piece of white paper or card to create the necessary illusion. The back of this card is coloured red all over. The third card is a genuine

Red and white on
the front - solid
red on reverse

Blue this side -
white on reverse

Air Mail card

white one on both sides, with an air-mail label obtainable from your local post office stuck on one side. This card should be placed, air-mail side towards your body, in your inside jacket pocket.

The other two cards are taken up and displayed in a fan as three cards. 'One red, one white and one blue.' The three (?) cards are now dropped into a hat or, for a different type of presentation, throw a borrowed handkerchief over the cards and hold them through the material.

Say that it is important that the audience should remember the colours of the cards. 'First there is the red one.' Take out the 'feke'* card, turning this over to show the plain red side to the audience. 'Then,' you say, 'there's the white one.' Lift up the remaining card with the white side towards the audience to show it. Place it back inside the hat. 'Then, finally, there's the blue one.' Now you remove this same card, blue side towards the audience. 'One blue card, one in the hat, one red.' The two cards are removed, shown, and placed aside. Finally the hat is tipped over to show the surprising disappearance of the white card which is supposed to be there.

As I have mentioned, if you wish, the cards can be covered with a handkerchief. Now the handkerchief is dramatically flicked into the air to show that the white card has gone!

Finally, reach into your inside pocket, pulling out the white card from there and, after a suitable pause, turn this over to show the gag tag-line.

I have described the effect as a pocket one with small-size cards. But of course, if the cards are made five or six times as large the effect can become a good one for platform use. The cards can be shown, then wrapped in a piece of news-

* 'Feke' is a term used by magicians. It is a secret aid, an unseen accessory.

paper, then withdrawn and shown. After some comedy by-play the white card vanishes and reappears under the back of your jacket, where the duplicate has been concealed all the time, held there by a paper clip suspended from a safety pin. Incidentally, a simple little holder of this type is a valuable accessory in many magical effects, enabling you easily to obtain a crumpled up ball of paper, a bank note, a card for production, and so on.

SPOOKY MATCHES

A neat pocket trick you'll get a lot of fun from! Six or more cards are shown and one is chosen. Cards are mixed together and placed in a row on the table. Magician now removes a couple of matches from a box and says these will represent his DIVINING STICKS. They are held together, that is side by side, between the right forefinger and thumb and passed over the cards. Suddenly, and in a very eerie, spooky manner the matches move apart. YES, they have correctly revealed the chosen card!

THE METHOD

The special gimmick which makes the trick possible is nothing more than a short piece of rubber tubing (cycle valve rubber) into which a match has been inserted from each end. Bend the tubing in half so that the matches come together and grip them as detailed, right thumb hiding the tubing which joins the matches together. Now if pressure on these two matches is relaxed ever so slightly they will begin to move, and as further pressure is relaxed they will eventually move right apart!

The moving of the matches is a fascinating effect, and when coupled with a divination of a chosen card, a baffling mystery.

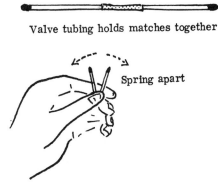

Valve tubing holds matches together

Spring apart

HOW TO KNOW THE SPECTATOR'S CARD

A number of methods are available and the performer can vary the method to suit the conditions under which he is performing.

Perfection method. From a borrowed pack have a number of cards, six or eight, dealt in a row on the table. Tell a spectator he is to pick up and look at any card. Whilst he is doing this you turn your back, but you glance round as though to see if he is following your instructions, NOTING THE POSITION OF THE MISSING CARD ON THE TABLE. Now, facing front, look at the back of this card and see what blemishes or imperfections you can find on it. It is not generally known but even in a new pack of cards every single card has some little blemish or mark that will make it distinctive to you. In a used pack your work is easy as you will see all manner of marks, creases, etc on the cards.

Ask the spectator to gather up the cards and to mix them up, placing them down in any order on the table. With your two matches begin passing them over cards haphazardly, one here, one there. Then, holding them over the card which

31

you recognise to be the chosen one, allow the matches to slowly move apart.

Easy method. Have six or so cards on the top of your pack in a prearranged order. They can be in a simple order like Ace, three, five, seven, nine, Jack. Cards can be false shuffled if you wish as long as top cards are kept intact. These cards are dealt face down in a row on to the table. Proceed as in the first method, glancing round and noting the card that is missing. You will instantly know the identity of this card. Have the cards collected up and dealt FACE UPWARDS on to the table, after being mixed up. It is easy to reveal the chosen card now.

Prepared method. With six cards of your own, mark them, placing a pencil dot on the back at different positions to indicate the value of the card. A spectator chooses one of the cards, you note which, then it is easy to pick this card out even though the cards are face down on the table.

Subtle Method. This is a clever method to use when you are performing at the dinner table. Place the cards out and contrive to get a few grains of salt on each. Have a spectator pick up and remember any card whilst your back is turned and replace it in the exact position it occupied previously. As you pass the matches over the cards it is easy for you to notice which card is without the tell-tale grains of salt!

I hope that you will have fun with 'Spooky Matches' and create mystery with them, too.

STRETCHING A SCARF

Here is a little novelty you will enjoy performing. It is so easy to do and yet it is quite an amazing effect. I recently fooled a colleague with it.

'I have a lot of trouble with my wife,' confides the

magician. 'Last Christmas she promised me something for my neck. I thought a nice scarf, instead she gave me a piece of rope. She treats me as a doormat; in fact, this year that is what she gave me (a doormat or a table mat or something like that). I really wanted a scarf so I shall stretch it—Actually some people think that I deserve a stretch . . . inside, but watch.'

Scarf formed
into 'Mat'

The magician picks up a small square of material which has a decorative fringe or braiding on each side. He holds this braiding between his hands, whirling the mat in the air, *and suddenly it stretches to several times its previous length!*

He puts the scarf around his neck and off he goes.

HERE'S HOW

The method is so simple as to be almost laughable. Use an ordinary tubular scarf, that is a scarf which is of double thickness. Most scarves are lined. The scarf does not have to have the same colour or material on both sides; for example, some scarves are yellow at the top and red underneath, and this is quite satisfactory for us. As my illustration shows, it is the tubular nature of the scarf which makes the trick possible.

Neatly and carefully the scarf is tucked in itself. Hold it about a foot from one end, opening the tubular scarf out and then working the rest of the material inside it until it resembles a small square of cloth.

In performance you pick up the small square of material, taking a firm grip on it so it does not open prematurely. Then take hold of the tasselled ends, one in each hand. With a swirling movement draw the hands apart, when the scarf will stretch to its full length.

CRAZY MATCHBOX

Magic has a number of 'backroom' boys. Names that mean nothing to the lay-public are honoured and revered by magicians all over the world. One such a character was the late Tom Sellers, a most prolific inventor of magical effects.

One small novelty of Tom's which always struck me as being rather amusing appeared in his book *Top Twenty*, published by the Supreme Magic Company. I have added a twist of my own to it that turns what was a clever optical illusion into a most appealing little 'quickie' to pull on your friends.

The magician removes from his pocket a box of matches. He pushes the tray or drawer of the matchbox, allowing

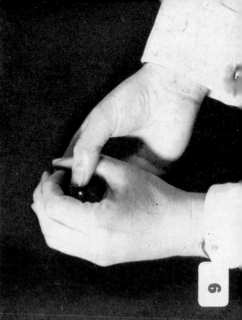

Page 35: Vanishing a billiard ball (6) *Right hand holds ball between the fingers and thumb;* (7) *left hand comes forward;* (8) *left hand fingers curl round the ball;* (9) *ball is completely encased*

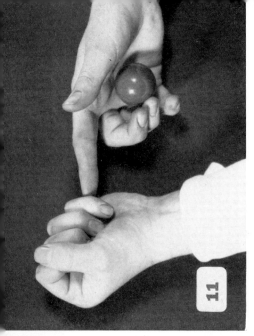

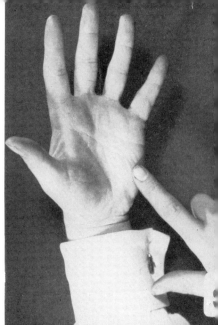

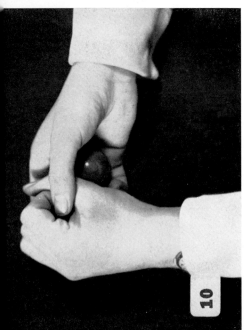

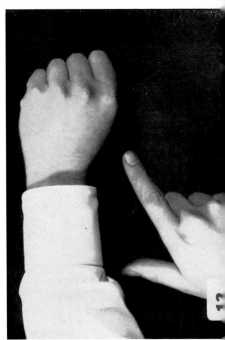

Page 36: Vanishing a billiard ball (10) *Note ball drops into right hand;* (11) *back view showing closed fist. Ball retained in right hand;* (12) *front view as audience see it;* (13) *hand opens to show the 'vanish'*

everything to be freely seen. The matches are tipped from the drawer on to the table. The drawer is placed back into the cover, where it just fits.

'Here's how to make something go a long way,' he says.

He pushes the drawer of the matchbox out a little way at one side, then pushes the drawer back again so that it is out at the opposite end, and again pushes it back with his forefinger with a tapping movement.

'Now it is at this end. It's here . . . it's there. Well, how can you explain *this*? It is at *both* ends *at the same time*!' He taps the drawer of the matchbox back and forward and to the surprise of the onlookers it is seen that, indeed, the drawer of the matchbox appears to be protruding from *both* sides of the matchbox at once.

The trick is over and the matchbox is put away . . . *but wait a moment*: 'I'll put the matches back,' says the magician. 'But first I'll show you that again! Watch! . . . you see it *this* side . . . you see it *that* side!' Again he moves the drawer of the matchbox back and forwards.

'Maybe you don't really believe your own eyes,' he says, 'well then, how can you explain *this*!' He lays the matchbox before him when it is seen that the drawer protrudes some half an inch *from each side*. Immediately he pushes out the drawer of the box, allowing everything to be examined.

HERE'S HOW

The first part of the effect is merely a clever optical illusion. If you hold the empty matchbox, which has a fairly loose fitting drawer (this is important), in front of you as illustrated, quickly tapping first one end and then the other a fantastic effect is obtained of *both* ends of the matchbox being visible at the same time!

But how about the climax to the effect?

The magician has prepared a duplicate matchbox with a

specially long drawer. I am afraid you will have to make this from cardboard or by making a composite drawer out

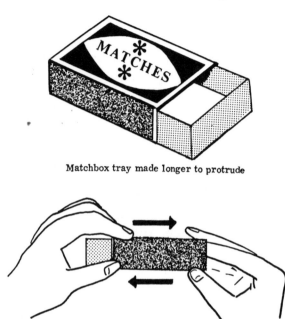

Matchbox tray made longer to protrude

Pushing tray backwards and forwards

of two drawers from two matchboxes. Not an insurmountable problem. The box with this extra long drawer is in your right-hand jacket pocket. Immediately you have performed the optical effect you place the first box into the pocket. Straight away drop it, and grab hold of the other matchbox, bringing it out and saying, 'Oh I must collect my matches—By the way, let me show you this little trick once more.' During this the fact that the matchbox protrudes at one end is hidden by the fingers, but now it is allowed to be seen as you tap the matchbox back and forwards through the cover. Finally pause, allowing the audience to see that they have been well and truly 'taken in', and lay the matchbox on the table.

LINKING CLIPS

The effect of magically linking articles together is a classic one. We have had 'Linking Rings', 'Linking Rope Rings', 'Linking Finger Rings', 'Linking Ribbons', and now here is a little pocket mystery using simple articles, ordinary 'trombone-type' paper clips.

From his pocket the performer removes a matchbox, opening this and displaying that inside it he has a number of ordinary paper clips. These are taken out and placed on the table and spread out where it is clearly seen that they are, in fact, completely single and separate.

Lifting the clips singly the magician drops them back into the matchbox until they are all inside. He closes the tray, giving the box a shake. The box is opened, the clips drop down on to the table but now they are all magically linked into a long chain!

HERE'S HOW

The method uses a matchbox which is feked by dividing the tray or drawer into two compartments with the aid of a strip of card taken from the end of a duplicate matchbox. The illustration shows that towards the end of one of these compartments a strong magnet is secured by glue or adhesive tape. The next requirement is a number of paper clips. Some of these (as many as you can get into the half matchbox, depending on the size—I use 15) are linked together into a chain whilst the other ones are left loose. Into the magnetic compartment go the loose links whilst the link chain lies hidden in the other compartment.

In performance, you show the matchbox and open the

tray halfway out revealing the compartment containing the loose clips. These clips are all over and concealing the magnet and you can allow the audience to see them

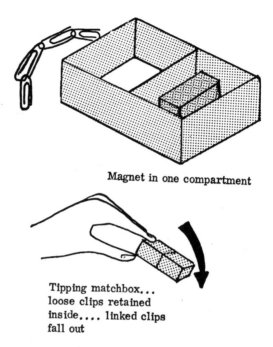

Magnet in one compartment

Tipping matchbox...
loose clips retained
inside.... linked clips
fall out

inside at this stage. Tilting the matchbox back towards yourself, remove the clips one at a time, with your finger-tips, dropping these on to the table. *Remember to tilt the box back away from the eye-level of the spectators so that they do not see the magnet inside the drawer.* If your chain of paper clips fills the second compartment and does not rattle about too much you will find that you are able to turn the matchbox over, thus supposedly emphasising that it is empty. The loose clips are picked up and dropped back into the box when immediately they cling to the magnet. Again it is possible to show the links inside, for they now cover the magnet. Close the tray, shaking the box, when the linked clips will rattle at one end. At the same time this movement ensures that all the loose clips are now firmly clinging to the magnet. Again open the tray half-way, this time revealing the half which contains the linked clips. Angling the matchbox away from the spectators push the drawer completely out of the box, now turning this over and allowing the clips in the box to fall out on to the table. The drawer, still upside down, is replaced in the cover and the matchbox is placed to one side. Now get hold of one of the clips on the table, slowly drawing this up and showing that all the clips are linked together.

Of course, the magical purist will wish to have a duplicate, unfeked matchbox in his pocket, switching the 'feke' one for this, so that after the clips have been examined by a spectator they can be put 'back into the matchbox' (now the ordinary one), thus leaving him 'all-clean' with nothing for the audience to discover.

THE MAGIC PENCIL

Here is a routine which will teach you magic, for it embodies several classic conjuring principles.

In performance the magician shows a long lead pencil. 'This is a magic pencil,' he asserts. 'It will write in any colour; I will prove it to you.' He takes up a small square of card, writing on this. 'First I will make it write red,' he says, 'then yellow, then green, and, finally, blue—There you are!'

He doesn't show the face of the card for a moment and the onlookers are naturally inquisitive. When he *does* turn the card over the audience find they have been well and truly 'had', for what he has written are just the *names* of the colours, all in black lead, one under the other.

'Maybe you are not impressed', says the magician, 'but I will continue and try to demonstrate the magic properties that the pencil possesses.'

He takes the plain card, slipping it inside a small pay envelope and laying this on the table before him. 'Watch the pencil,' he says, as he performs a crazy balancing feat. For now the pencil is balanced at a crazy angle on the extended forefinger. The pencil is taken and held in the loosely-clenched hand. Suddenly it rises up to the fingers! 'The pencil is becoming too active,' says the magician; 'I shall have to wrap it up.' He rolls the pencil up in a piece of paper. 'Although it is more restrained it still possess its magical powers,' he continues. He touches the envelope on the table with the rolled-up package. 'We don't need the pencil any more,' he says, as he crushes the package up. The pencil has vanished and the crumpled paper is pocketed.

The magician tears open the envelope and removes from it one card. There is nothing else inside the envelope. There, written on the card are the colours red, yellow, green, and blue, just as previously but with this difference. *Each word is now written in the colour which it names*!

HERE'S HOW

Again, to make things easy for you, I will break the working down into a number of different phases. First of all the appearance of the words in colour on the card.

The illustration will show that already inside the pay envelope is a double card made from two cards fastened together with cellotape around three edges. Cellotape is on the *inside* and again my drawing will show how this is applied. The two cards are fastened along a long edge and cellotape is placed on the other long edge and on the bottom. The edges of the tape are folded inwards, the two cards then being pressed together. You have made what is, in fact, an open-ended sheath.

Written on the outside of the sheath are the four words, each with a coloured crayon, 'red' with red crayon, 'yellow'

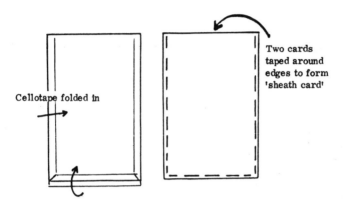

Cellotape folded in

Two cards taped around edges to form 'sheath card'

with yellow crayon, 'green' with green crayon, and 'blue' with blue crayon. This card is already inside the small pay envelope, the open end being at the top.

The card which you show at the start of the routine has been cut a little smaller than the sheath card so that it will slide inside it. Don't be worried that this difference in size will ever be noticed. *It won't*, principally because of the time lapse in the showing of the two cards.

In performance, you pick up the pay envelope and open the flap, pressing in on the sides of the envelope, which will automatically open the sheath card up. Show the card on which you have just written with black pencil and place this inside the envelope *and directly into the sheath card*. Make sure that you push it right down. The envelope can be sealed up or merely tossed down on the table. When you remove the card the next time you remove the double one. Produce it blank side up, then turn it over to show the surprising climax of the coloured writing. The envelope can be torn up.

That accounts for part 1 of our mystery. But how about the peculiar antics of the pencil? Well, the pencil is not quite as innocent as it appears. A long brightly-coloured

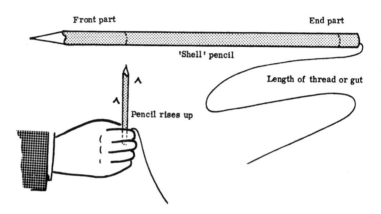

one, it is really a tube of glossy flint paper. This is rolled around a rod or pencil and glued at the edge to form a removable tube. This tube is then pulled off the rod and a short piece of pencil is glued in at one end to represent one end of a pencil and a longer piece, about an inch or more long, at the other end with a sharpened point to represent the genuine end of the pencil.

Obviously, you will be able to write carefully with this pencil, and also when you place this on your finger, the pointed side resting on the finger, the pencil will balance there as, in fact, this is the heavier end. One other little preparation. Before the end of the pencil (that is, the end opposite the point), is stuck into position, a length of fine thread or hair about eighteen inches long is pushed in with it so that the end of this is trapped there. This thread hangs loose and is unseen during the routine.

The Working. Let us run through the basic effect. You show the plain card, writing on it. Be careful how you handle the pencil as you do not wish this to become prematurely bent. Then show the card, placing this into the envelope and directly into the sheath. Balance the pencil on your forefinger, next form the right hand into a fist, pushing the pencil in. You will find that the length of hair hangs over the hand. Take hold of this with the left hand. As you slowly move the hands apart so the pencil will rise out of the fingers. This is quite a spooky stunt and can be repeated several times.

Now wrap the pencil, thread and all, inside a piece of paper. Touch the package against the envelope then crush the package up and pocket it. The pencil has apparently vanished. Finally display the card in the envelope.

There are a few little subtle points which you might like to incorporate into the routine. You can have a duplicate crushed up piece of paper inside your pocket and pull this out later. Also, if you wish, you can have a duplicate unprepared pencil in your jacket pocket for later display.

If you will think around the *principles* I have given you here you will see how these can be adapted to other effects. A bamboo cane, a stick of rock, a magic wand, *can rise from the fingers,* can be made to *vanish,* and so on; and a message can appear on a blank card, a plain card can change into a playing card, and all sorts of novel adaptations are possible, using the basic magical principles of the *sheath,* of the *thread* (used in levitation and suspension), and the '*shell*' (hollow paper shape) which resembles the real article and can be easily vanished.

THE X-RAY MACHINE

The following is not only a novel card discovery but

also incorporates the ghostly appearance of spooky writing —the name of a selected card.

The plot is simple, the working is simple, but the trick is very effective. The mentalist comes forward and offers the spectator a selection from a deck of cards, requesting him to look at it and finally place it face down upon the table in front of him. When this is done, the mentalist displays a square frame made in wood or cardboard. This, he explains, is his new X-ray machine, complete with a little cover, also displayed. A small sheet of plain white cardboard is now shown and is examined by any of the audience, the magician asking a member to place his signature on one of the corners to make sure that it is the same piece used throughout the experiment.

The frame is placed upon the card, and the cover closed over the frame. 'The Spirits are at work!' says the performer. 'They are delving into your brain and will cause an image of the selected card to appear on this examined blank piece of cardboard.'

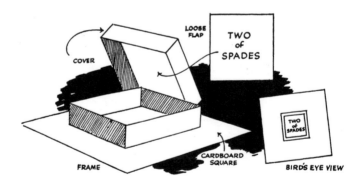

When the cover is removed, there on the cardboard inside the frame of the X-ray machine is written or drawn (a little scrawly, but legible, and true enough) the name of the selected card!

To obtain this effect, I employ three old principles and from them create a new effect.

HERE'S HOW

The illustration shows the required apparatus, which is extremely easy to make—merely a little frame measuring about 2 in square, and a fit-on cover which has a flat top. Up inside this lid is hidden a loose fitting flap of cardboard. One side of this flap is plain white and on this is some scribbled writing, naming the playing card which you will be 'forcing' on to the spectator later. The other (outside) of the flap matches the inside of the lid. You will also require a square of white cardboard, a little larger than but matching the colour and texture of the secreted flap.

The working is simple and shouldn't be too hard to follow. Have the sheet of cardboard, the little frame, and the cover top, lying upon your table ready for use. First display the little frame, explaining that it is a new type of X-ray machine which you have just created, and also show the cover (which has the secreted flap up inside). Next, the sheet of plain cardboard is shown and examined by spectators, the magician asking one to initial or sign over the corner. When this is done, the cardboard square is placed flat upon the table, and the performer places the frame in the centre of this. At this stage the spectators may look inside the frame, when the performer displays it for the last time. The cover is now shown and placed over the frame, the flap falling down inside, and the cover keeps everything nicely concealed. The deck of cards is shown, and the spectator has a free choice. That's what it looks like from the audience's point of view! However, the per-

47

former actually *forces* the card upon the spectator. There are many different methods of doing this, and I will detail an easy one later. When the card has been selected (forced), the performer goes through some hocus pocus, stating that the spirits have arrived and are at this moment in presence.

When the spectator is asked to remove the cover, he will see that the writing has appeared, this being, of course, the writing on the inside flap, which now rests inside the frame, and which, due to the matching colour, looks like part of the larger sheet of cardboard. The writing, of course, names the chosen card, which makes the effect even more baffling.

Here is a simple way of Forcing a Card.

Simplicity Force. This is a very cheeky, but surprisingly effective, way of forcing a card. Have the force card at the top of the pack. Ask someone to give you a small number and quickly count off that number of cards, REVERSING THEIR ORDER AS YOU DO SO. Place the cards on the table, and say that you are going to use 'the chosen card—the bottom card of the packet'. In actual fact, this is the card which was originally at the top. In theory it all sounds rather 'bald', but in practice you will find this method surprisingly effective.

For good measure here's another easy method.

Crossing the Cut. Have the force card at the bottom of the pack. Ask someone to cut the pack in two. Pick up the bottom packet of cards and place it across at an angle on the top of the other packet, saying that you are doing this to mark the cut. Stress that the spectator cut the cards anywhere he wished, and that you did not influence him in any way. Then say that you are going to use the 'cut at' card. Still keeping the packet face down, lift the top packet off and slide off the bottom card. This is your force card.

BARE HAND CARD CATCH

For some time past I have performed this effect with some success and on the occasions that I have worked before an audience of magicians, invariably I have been approached afterwards and asked 'Who sells this prop?' The answer has been 'No one'. I have decided to release it for our readers' benefit, and feel sure you will enjoy working this fine effect.

No doubt readers will have seen magicians 'catching' chosen cards on swords, umbrellas, daggers, wands, etc, but here is a non-sleight method using only the BARE HANDS!

EFFECT

A pack of playing cards is removed from its case, displayed, and the cards shuffled. One is selected and noted. It is returned to the pack by spectators, and the pack returned to its case. The performer holds up the case containing the pack high above his head and, giving the case a shake, the contents fall and scatter. The magician reaches out and catches a card . . . yes, you're quite correct, it is the CHOSEN CARD!

HERE'S HOW

You lucky chaps! The 'necessary' needed for this excellent effect is inexpensive and easily made—even the non 'Do-It-Yourself' merchants will be able to make this up! You want a pack of playing cards and the case that goes with it. It is necessary to have a duplicate of one of the cards in the pack. This duplicate card is smeared with MELROSE (hand tablet) or even a smear of softish soap will do, on its face side. The card that is generally fixed to the back of the card case, and displays the back design of the cards, is also smeared with MELROSE or soap. The duplicate card is placed over the fixed card adhering to the case, so that to the spectators it appears to be merely a 'card case'. The audience will hardly notice the case—this is just incidental. All the performer has to do is to 'force' the twin of the duplicate card now stuck on the card case on to a spectator. A simple yet effective method of doing this is

Front

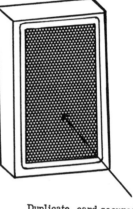

Duplicate card secured by soap or wax onto back of card case

to have the duplicate card face down on top of the pack. Shuffle the cards with an overhand shuffle, retaining the top card in place by pressure of the fingers. Now angle the pack back slightly, drawing the top card back an inch into the hand. From the front of the deck start to draw out and deal cards from 'the top' on to the table without disturbing the drawn-back card on the top until the cry of 'Stop' is called. Then deal the next card (*really* the top card) on to the table and show it. The spectator may himself replace the card in the pack and shuffle it.

Alternatively, use one of the 'forces' described in 'The X-ray Machine' (p 45). The pack of cards is inserted into the card case—about halfway in—and held with the open end pointing towards the floor. With a swinging movement the cards will fall and scatter from the case and under cover of the falling cards, the performer slides off the duplicate card from the back of the card case. The case is allowed to fall to the floor just a fraction of a second after you have 'caught' the chosen card in mid-air, and are proudly holding it in view for verification.

GHOSTLY CARDS

Here's a visual card trick which can be presented on stage or at fairly close-up sessions.

The performer displays two playing cards, freely, front and back. Then, holding a card in each hand, he passes one card slowly and deliberately through the other! Truly a unique magical effect. One card is seen to dissolve right through the centre of the other, to be removed from the back! At the end the cards are again shown to be ordinary playing cards.

KNOW-HOW

The method is very simple and requires no skill to perform. You require a specially prepared card, which has an extra portion of card fastened loosely to it. As our illustration shows, the duplicate piece of card is cut rather unevenly, and is attached at the top and bottom. You also require another card for the penetration, and an unprepared duplicate of the feked card.

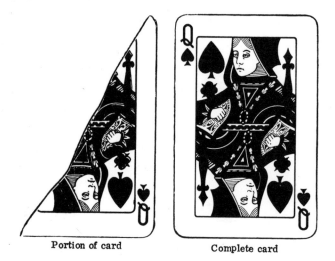

Portion of card   Complete card

In presenting the trick, have the unprepared duplicate in your right-hand jacket pocket. Other cards are on the table or on top of a matching pack.

Show the feked card and the ordinary card back and front. The clever feking makes it possible for the performer to work at close quarters, and the fact that a court card is used hides any join in the pattern. The cards should be kept on the move during the presentation of the effect and

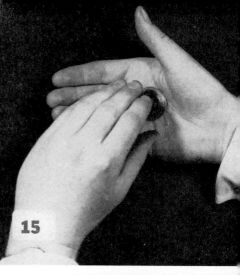

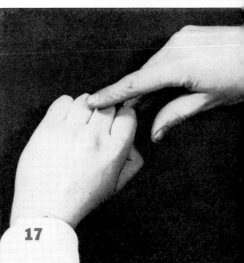

age 53: Take-away vanish (14) *Coin is
esting on palm of hand;* (15) *left hand
omes over to lift it away;* (16) *hand is
osed into a fist. Right hand starts to turn
ver;* (17) *right hand now turned and points
) left;* (18) *left hand opens slowly to
reveal it is empty*

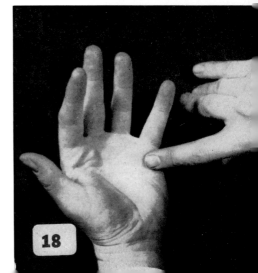

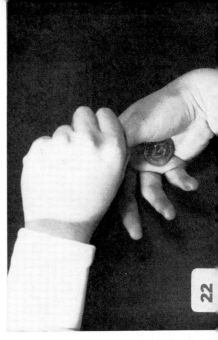

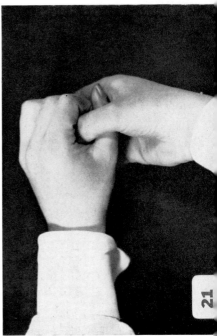

Page 54: A round-about vanish (19) Coin placed into left fist; (20) right hand gets ready to push it inside; (21) coin pushed in, drops into right hand; (22) back view showing coin is secretly held before the 'vanish'

care should be taken as to the angle of light. With both cards backs upwards you advance to a spectator and ask him to note that there is definitely no break or tear in the cards. Needless to say you should retain your hold on the cards during this casual check.

Now rub the feked card against the face of the other card, and as you do so allow the edge to slide under the loose piece. Continue to slide the card through diagonally and remove it, apparently from the back. To the audience it will appear as though the cards have mysteriously passed through each other.

When you are performing close up and it is an advantage to have your 'props' examined, drop both the cards into your jacket pocket. As an afterthought, or upon the request to 'show us the cards', you remove the two unprepared cards for examination.

'Ghostly Cards' will be found to be the perfect little novelty to include with almost any card effects as an 'aside'. It looks impossible and yet, like all good tricks, it's easy when you know how.

3

More Ambitious Problems

INEXPENSIVE NEWSPAPER SILKS PLUS

THE title of the effect explains that this method of producing silks (small silk handkerchiefs) from a newspaper is cheap to make, but it also has the benefit of a different and unusual climax which in the end gets rid of the 'gimmick'.

EFFECT

A piece of newspaper is shown on both sides and holes are punctured in various parts of it. From these are materialised coloured silks, and they are shown to be protruding from both sides.

After producing these, the magician feels like a smoke so he reaches through the paper and produces a cigarette, but finds that he has no matches. Puncturing another hole in the sheet, he produces a matchbox and removes a match to light his well earned cigarette.

APPARATUS REQUIRED

What could be cheaper? . . . A used matchbox, which is simply and easily prepared by cutting one end off the tray.

The tray is placed back in position minus its end, and into it are loaded several small silks. It is surprising just how many you can push inside. Around the matchbox is placed a flesh-coloured elastic band which has two purposes —(1) to hold a cigarette against the side of the box, and (2) to fasten the box to the back of the fingers.

One final thing you must do: that is to jam a match between the tray and drawer of the box ready to be pulled out when required. With the box already loaded and upon your table, on top of which is placed the newspaper sheet, you are all set for the presentation.

PRESENTATION

As the left hand goes to pick up the paper, the right hand middle fingers enter into the elastic band and this, as the illustration clearly shows, fixes the box to the back of the hand with the opening pointing towards the finger-tips. The sheet is now held in the right hand, whilst the left keeps turning it over, showing all sides. The gimmick is out of sight and you will find there is plenty of cover.

When you want to produce a silk, the fingers of the right hand curl inwards allowing the box also to point against the sheet. A hole is punctured at this position and the silk is withdrawn from the box right through the paper. When fully out, the sheet can be reversed to show it on both sides, the gimmick again going back in its original position on the back of the hand.

This is done several times. After all the silks have been produced from the paper, and the box is empty, the magician remarks that he could do with a smoke. Puncturing another hole somewhere in the paper, the left hand pulls out the cigarette (away from the side of the box) and puts this between his lips.

Looking for some matches, he decides to produce these

also, and through a further hole produces the matchbox, leaving the elastic band in the hand. You will find in most cases it will remain around the centre finger. With the

Handkerchiefs loaded inside box—
cigarette behind rubber band,
match jammed between
drawer and tray

open end

Secured matchbox on back of hand.
Secretly held behind newspaper

single match being jammed between the tray and drawer, you will find it an easy matter to extract it and light the cigarette.

You are left entirely clean with no metal gimmicks to ditch, and with a different climax to the standard effect, which always did seem to lack one.

IN THE GLASS APPEARANCE

Simplicity is certainly the keynote of this effect, for the apparatus used can be obtained in just a minute: all that is required is one normal glass tumbler and a pack of cards.

EFFECT

A card is selected from a deck of cards. It is looked at, then returned to the pack. After displaying a clear tumbler, the performer places the pack inside the glass. The glass with the pack inside is inverted, then the cards fall to the floor, except for one and, need I say it, it is indeed the chosen card.

WORKING AND PRESENTATION

The secret of the effect is so simple that you may think it is not the sort of thing you should present in your act; but you would be wrong. The effect is good and that is what really matters.

A card is selected from the pack, then the performer cuts the deck and asks the spectator to return it somewhere in the centre. When it has been replaced, the performer keeps a break with his little finger. From the audience's point of view the card is somewhere in the centre of the deck. The cards are cut, bringing the chosen card to the top of the pack. At this stage a false shuffle would be ideal, giving the audience the impression that it is truly mixed up amongst the others. (Merely retain the card in place with the finger-tips during a casual overhand shuffle.)

The pack is placed inside the glass, which is held in the right hand. Whilst placing the deck right inside the glass, push the top card (chosen one) down further than the others, allowing it to be 'jammed' against both sides of the glass. When the glass is inverted, the left hand holds the pack inside at this stage.

The spectator is asked to call out the name of his selected card, and, at the same time, the pack is allowed to fall to the floor, or scatter into a hat, which may be on the table.

One card will remain inside the glass, the chosen one, which has been jammed in position; and its appearance gives a splendid effect.

Pack falls,
Chosen card is
retained

In another method of presentation the performer holds the glass of cards in his right hand and simply makes an upward motion with it, allowing the cards to shoot right up into the air and leaving the chosen card in view inside the glass. Whichever way you wish to present the trick, I can assure you it goes over extremely well.

PRANKY PAPERS

Here's a trick which blends two well known magical principles to make a surprising little pocket mystery.

The magician shows four squares of tissue paper. Let us say, one red, one yellow, one green, and one blue. Each of the tissue papers is crumpled up into a ball. The magician turns his back on the audience, holding his hands behind him. His cupped right hand rests on his left hand.

A spectator is invited to pick up any one of the coloured pieces of paper and drop it into the magician's hand, and then to hide the other three pieces.

The magician turns to the front, places a hand to his forehead (to aid his concentration) and announces the colour of the paper he holds!

This mystifying stunt is repeated several times.

'Let us go a little further,' the conjurer says. 'This time when I turn around I want you to place into my hand *all* the four balls of paper, mixing these up so that it is impossible for me to tell one from the other.'

Again he turns to face the front. 'Now name a colour,' he demands.

Whatever colour the audience names the magician is instantly able to produce it from behind his back. This is repeated three times, the remaining ball of paper then being also placed before him.

'I think you will agree that you have seen a very good trick', says the magician. 'Unfortunately, there is not much *money* in it, that is, of course, unless you happen to be a *real* magician!' He picks up the first ball of paper and tears it away, and from it produces a silver coin. *One by one coins appear from each of the balls of paper!* 'That's how to make money,' he says as he pockets the four gleaming coins.

HERE'S HOW

There are really *eight* squares of tissue paper involved (each 4 or 5 in square) and four of these have a coin in

61

the centre. The paper is crumpled around the coin so its presence is hidden. Each of these balls of paper is suspended under the rear edge of the jacket on a hairpin (bobby-pin), held in place by a safety pin, as shown in my illustration.

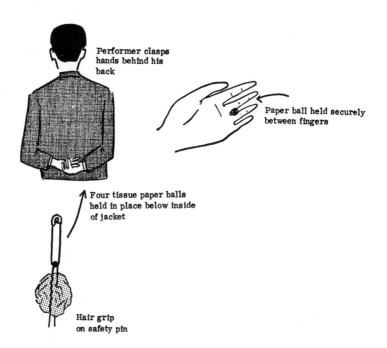

Performer clasps hands behind his back

Paper ball held securely between fingers

Four tissue paper balls held in place below inside of jacket

Hair grip on safety pin

The other four pieces of paper are unprepared. Crumple these into four balls, placing them on the table, then turn around as detailed. As soon as the ball of paper has been put into your hand, close it, swinging round to face the front. Behind the back, the right hand opens, the left hand moves up, tears off a tiny piece of tissue paper, clipping this between the fingers. The left hand now comes to the front and moves up to the brow as you appear to be in deep concentration. You will find it an easy matter to see the colour of the small piece of paper as the hand moves up in front of the face to the forehead. Naming the colour, bring the right hand to the front, placing the ball of paper it contains in front of you. The small snippet of paper in the left hand is easily and quietly pocketed in the outside jacket pocket.

This process is repeated.

Finally, when all the four balls of paper have been dealt with, gather them together and push them into your hip pocket, so both hands are now empty. One at a time pull down the coloured balls of paper as they are called for by the audience, laying these on the table, then finally bringing the last ball of paper to the front. You are all set for the surprising denouement. Showing that your hands are unmistakably empty you pick up the first paper, tearing this open and allowing a silver coin to fall in front of you on the table or into a glass which is there to receive it, and one by one the four coins magically materialise.

TELEVISION ACES

A classic of conjuring is the 'Four Ace Trick' and here is my method, using no feked cards or feked apparatus and presented under the fairest conditions possible.

The routine I offer here is my own, as is the idea of the 'Television Folder'. If you will take a little time to study the working and to learn the sequence of events I feel sure that you will be delighted at the cleanness and the logic behind everything you do. No elaborate moves or sleights of any kind are used and in fact NONE need be used at all! Try the effect through with a pack of cards in your hand, and I know you'll be convinced that here is something really worthwhile and baffling to any audience.

HERE'S HOW

The only properties required are an ordinary pack of cards and the television folder (easily made from cardboard). You can use any cards.

The pack is set up as follows. First pick out the four aces from the pack, then the following cards; the five of clubs, the three of diamonds and the five of hearts. Next pick out all the SPADES from the pack.

With the cards before you lay them out like this: first the four aces, together, *face up* on the table. The ace of diamonds, clubs, hearts and spades. On top of these cards place the three of Diamonds, five of clubs and five of hearts. On top of these cards deal any NINE CARDS, then on top of these place all the spades. The balance of the pack goes

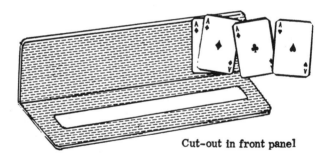

Cut-out in front panel

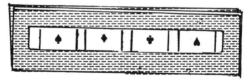

Centres of '3s' and
'5s' show as Aces

on top, and the cards are replaced in their case.

The folder, which gives the trick new interest, also makes it easy for you! In fact this just consists of a plain white cardboard backing sheet, and a wood-grain finish cardboard front cut out so that the back shows through, like a white 'screen'.

When the aces are placed along the folder and this is tilted up, the *centre pips only* of the cards show through. The size of the folder is $13\frac{1}{2}$ in x 4 in and the cut-out is $11\frac{1}{2}$ in x $1\frac{1}{4}$ in, both pieces being hinged together so they open like a book. The illustrations will make the construction quite clear. It is quite easy to make. Your deck is set. So let's get on with the working.

Working. Show the folder. Open it up and lay it open on the table. Remove the pack of cards from its case. Fan the cards out. Close the fan (cards are only fanned momentarily, so don't worry about the spades being all together). The pack is turned face downwards and the top four cards are pushed off and shown. They are the four aces. The cards are given to a spectator to examine. Whilst he is looking at the aces run over the top three cards from the left hand which is holding the pack, to the right. The cards are then squared up but so that a break is held with the fleshy ball of the left index finger and the top three cards are raised slightly. Apparently you have merely toyed idly with the cards whilst the aces were examined. The four aces are now taken from the spectator in your right hand. If the cards are not in the correct order then rearrange them, keeping them face upwards—diamond, club, heart, and spade. The cards are rested MOMENTARILY on the 'top of the pack' whilst you indicate the folder on the table. Immediately the four cards are removed PLUS THE THREE FROM ABOVE THE BREAK. The pack is placed down on the table and the seven cards are held squared up and face down between the hands.

Alternative. Even this simple 'move' (if it can be called

such) can be dispensed with if desired. At the start merely show the four aces in a fan, the three other cards being behind the ace of diamonds and squared up so that they are unseen. The fan of cards is shown and dropped on to the top of the pack. Then they are dealt straightway on to the folder. In my opinion this is by no means as good as the working previously detailed, but I have mentioned it here for the sake of completeness.

Patter. 'I should like to introduce you to this model of the latest invention . . . *Panoramic Television*— The television with the wide screen. You sit at one end of the screen and your wife sits at the other and you tell each other what's happening at your end! You tell each other what's going on—or in the case of a French Revue what's coming off!

'You will notice that this model has no works. That's because I'm buying it on the HP. We had the aerial last month. We shall be viewing by Christmas! Isn't that horrible!' (Hold the open folder up and look through the cut-out.) 'You see some horrible things on television don't you. It's all right! You look just as horrible from here!' (In mock TV voice) 'This programme is unsuitable for Children!

'Maybe the first thing we'll see when our television is installed will be a conjurer performing a card trick' (remove cards from their case). 'This is a trick that has already been performed several times on television. This evening perhaps you'll see how you . . . the *trick* I mean . . . is done! It's called a 'Four Ace Trick' and naturally we use the four aces —that's logical isn't it! A snap of my fingers and here they are at the top!' (This is quite effective if you can manage a false shuffle of the few face cards before you reveal the aces.) 'Perhaps you'd like to examine the aces, sir, resisting the natural temptation to slip a couple of them up your sleeve. You've certainly got a winning hand there!

'May I have the cards? Thank you. You're quite satisfied, I hope? And if you're not I'd be very much obliged
if you would . . . keep your mouth shut and stay where
you are! You've seen FACES on television, now we're going
to put the ACES on the television . . . just along here . . . but
before I do that I should like to tell you something about
these aces.'

Working (continued). Holding the cards squared up and
face down in the left hand lift the top card, the ace of diamonds, show it, and place it on the bottom of the stack.
Tilt the cards in the hands to show the ace there and 'all
fair'. Show the ace of clubs in the same way and place it
on the bottom. Also the ace of hearts. The ace of spades
is shown and replaced ON THE TOP OF THE PACKET. Making
it quite obvious that you do not interfere with the cards in
any way, drop them on to the top of the pack whilst you
adjust the position of the folder. Then deal the four cards
from the top along in a line, face downwards so that the
centres of the cards come over the cut-out of the screen.
Returning to the beginning of the row deal three cards on
the top of each ace. Unknown to the audience this will
really bring all the aces together on top of the ace of spades.
Place the pack to one side and 'tidy' the four piles of cards.
Then close the folder and tip it so that the 'aces' show
through the screen. What the audience really sees is the
genuine ace of spades and the centre pips of the two fives and
the three, these exactly representing the aces that should be
there. The folder is tilted back and a spectator is asked to
select any of the cards remaining in the pack. Fan the cards
before him, making sure that he takes one of the top cards
(all spades). Explain to him that the suit of the card he takes
is to determine which ace he is to have . . . you will use the
cards at that position. Whilst he is looking at his chosen
card and you are explaining things to him casually, give the

cards an overhand shuffle to break up their arrangement. Then lay the pack to one side.

Note. If you use the *alternative* method of working the procedure of showing the aces etc will of course have been dispensed with.

Patter. 'Each of these aces has a special and highly significant meaning. For example the ace of diamonds is supposed to represent great wealth and riches. The ace of clubs denotes travel. Choose this card and you'll go a long way! I chose this card the other day and I heard someone say, "Well as far as I'M concerned the further HE goes the better!" That really hurt my feelings. I said, "Let me tell you I'm a very fooling Magician." "Yes," the chap said, "you sure fooled me, I THOUGHT YOU WERE GOING TO BE GOOD!

'The ace of hearts is the LOVE card. Choose this card—and be careful; Maybe a romance will come back into your life. And be sure to look under the bed before getting into it! I did last night—and there were two beautiful girls there! I said, "You have five minutes for ONE of you to get out of here." Well, I mean to say, I was tired! If ever I get married they'll have to throw VITAMIN PILLS instead of CONFETTI!

'Last of all, there's the ace of spades. Some people wrongly believe that this card is unlucky, a superstition that sprang up because in olden times a duty was imposed on packs of cards through this card, which was printed only under Government supervision. Persons caught printing their own ace of spades were shot! Well, that was unlucky for *them* I'll agree, but many a fortune has been made, many a gamble has paid off, and paid off well, at the turn of the black ace. For them it has been the luckiest card in the pack! So there they are. The four aces. I shall not touch or tamper with the cards in any way, but deal them there.

Birds of a feather, all in a row! Three we are told is a Magic Number so let us place three cards on the top of each ace, three cards here, there, and there. I wonder if you can remember the order of the aces? Spades, diamonds, clubs and hearts—all are on view along the Panoramic Screen!

'If I were to ask someone to choose one of these aces your own personal prejudices and wishes would enter in the selection, so to make the choice 100 per cent fair perhaps someone would like to remove any one of the remaining cards in the pack. If you choose a heart we will use the ace of hearts, if a diamond the ace of diamonds. What was the suit of your freely chosen card? A spade. Right. We will use the pile of cards with the ace of spades. The other cards and aces we'll gather up. I'm sorry I can't congratulate you—YOU'VE chosen the pile washed in BRAND X!'

Working (continued). Gather up the three rejected piles of cards. Spread the remaining four cards along the folder and close it. Twelve cards are now held face down in the hand, in one pile. Now you can either slip a card from the top of the pile to the bottom, or else you can merely lift off one card from the top of the packet whilst you are pattering and replace it on the bottom. That's up to you! You do this so when you turn the cards over, the three or fives do not show at the fourth position to give the audience the tiniest clue as to the 'modus operandi'. Turn over the top three cards of the packet, tossing them on to the table. Snap the top card of the packet and dramatically turn it over. It is is NOT an ace! The ace has gone! Repeat this with all the cards, showing that all the aces have vanished. (This is much better than merely running through all the cards at once.) Well 'point' the vanish, as though the aces are vanishing as you snap the cards with your fingers. Finally turn the folder completely over to show the aces again on view through the cut-out screen and then fold back the front to show the aces fully. Everything may be left to be examined.

Patter. 'Now for the MAGIC! One, two, three, cards—a snap of the fingers—a pass—and quicker than you can say, "Stand clear! . . . SSSCHWEPPES tonic water", the ace has gone! I'll do that again! One, two, three, cards. Now for the mime—Snap—Crackle—but no pop—what DOES that make me?—and the ace has gone!

'Two from three leaves one. Watch it go, one, two, three . . . it's gone. And here they are! Birds of a feather flock TOGETHER . . . the four aces!'

That's it! I hope you'll like it and have as much fun with it as I have had.

THE DIVINING STICKS

Here's a novel trick for stage or close-up performances, one which is mystifying and unusual.

The magician invites a member of the audience to help him and to participate in an unusual experiment. The spectator is to act as the committee man on behalf of the audience, ensuring that all is fair and 'above board'.

Five ordinary tumblers are on the magician's table together with a jug containing some water. After the spectator has satisfied himself that everything is as it should appear, he pours some water into one of the glasses, any one of his choice. The magician shows a number of paper bags, placing one of these over the glass of water and asking the spectator to please continue doing this with the other bags. Each paper bag is opened and placed mouth downwards over a glass, so it acts as a cover for it. It is pressed tightly down so there is no possibility of the magician being

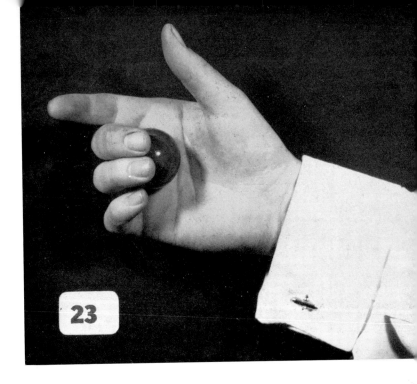

Page 71 : A simple palm (23) *Rear view showing palmed ball;*
(24) *front view of hand*

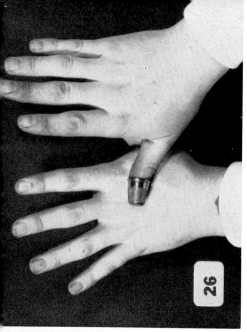

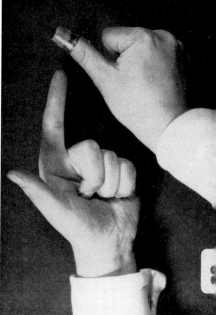

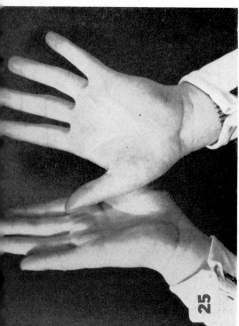

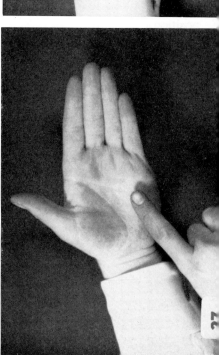

Page 72: **Producing a thimble** (25) *Both hands being shown empty;* (26) *rear view showing concealed thimble on right hand thumb;* (27) *right hand closed ready to point at left;* (28) *right hand thumb released showing production of thimble*

able to peek underneath it. Next the magician shows a couple of rough wooden twigs, which he explains are divining sticks used by a water diviner. The magician states that he has the uncanny power of being able to locate the presence of liquid with the aid of the sticks. The sticks are handed to a member of the audience to examine.

Now as the magician turns (so that it is obvious he cannot see the covered glasses on his table), the spectator who has been assisting is invited to move the glasses around. He has to handle them *carefully* so as not to splash or soil the bag covering the water, and to move them around in such a way that the audience are confused as to the whereabouts of the glass of water. (He himself, of course, will know the position owing to its extra weight.) When the spectator has finished moving the glasses around he has to call 'Ready'.

The magician turns round and collects the two wooden sticks, holding these together in his hand. He passes the sticks over each of the glasses in turn. WHEN THE TWIGS ARE HELD OVER THE GLASS CONTAINING THE WATER THESE IMMEDIATELY MOVE ABOUT AND DRAW APART!

The magician tests the reaction with the sticks several times, always with the same results. '*This* glass,' he claims, 'contains the water.' The glasses are all uncovered, and, sure enough, he is revealed to be correct. All remaining glasses can be shown and the two sticks can be minutely examined. The magician's hands are empty with no concealed gimmicks of any kind.

HERE'S HOW

The secret is both simple and subtle, all the apparatus being easily obtainable. Two questions have to be answered. (1) How does the magician know under which bag the water is hidden? (2) What is the motive power for the two sticks?

The answer to the first question is easy. Use ordinary quarter pound biscuit bags or fruit bags, which you can obtain from your grocer. If you examine these bags you will find that most of them have a serrated edge, a peculiarity of their manufacture. One of the bags is simply feked. A few of the serrated edges are drawn up with the fingertips and then with scissors trimmed along straight. Thus, this bag, to you, is immediately distinguishable from the others.

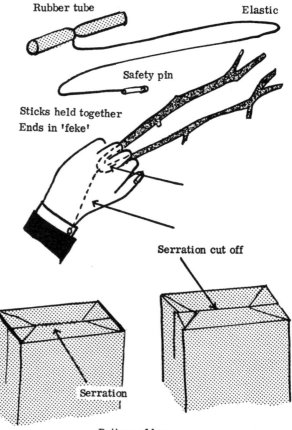

Rubber tube

Elastic

Safety pin

Sticks held together
Ends in 'feke'

Serration cut off

Serration

Bottom of bag

Alternatively any simple mark can be used—a small piece cut away, a crease put in the fold, or a pencil dot put on a strategic point. However the method we have given is preferable, for this is *natural* feking of the bag. There is nothing whatsoever for the audience to discover, furthermore when the glasses are covered by the bags the bottom of the bags are immediately and quickly visible, even although the 'body' of the bags may have been drawn in tightly around the glasses. So much then for the first part of our problem. How about the second part?

On p 30 I describe a clever little stunt with two matches which are held together and yet when you wish slowly draw apart. This is the principle used here, but in rather a novel way. First of all obtain a small piece of metal spring or surgical rubber tubing 2-3 in long. Around the centre of this piece of tubing tie a length of cord elastic, and at the other end of this fasten an ordinary safety pin. This 'gimmick' (to use a conjuring term) is pinned inside the right sleeve so that the piece of tubing is actually a few inches up the sleeve and completely out of sight. The two twigs which you use are unprepared and have been taken from a hedgerow or from your neighbour's garden. It may be necessary to trim the sticks, for they should fit into the ends of the tubing easily.

Working. In an earlier chapter I stressed that good tricks should be simple, enabling you to concentrate on presentation. This is a good example of this type of mystery. Build the effect up with a short discourse about water divining and how a great uncle of yours was clever in this respect. The twigs, you explain, belonged to him. They do possess an uncanny power and you will try it out this evening. You now proceed, as I have explained, getting a spectator to assist, having him pour liquid into one glass, then covering all the glasses over.

You take up the prepared bag, placing this over the glass of water as though illustrating how it should be done. The spectator continues, and you can help him if you wish to speed the operation up. Then the spectator moves the glasses around according to your instructions. While he is doing this, turn to one side, and you will find it an easy matter to insert your left hand into your right sleeve, getting hold of the length of tubing there and drawing it down into the palm of the right hand. When the spectator has finished with his manoeuvres, you turn round, taking the two sticks and inserting them, one on each side, into the right hand, which you hold back uppermost and in a fist (really into the gimmick). When the sticks are firmly in position inside the tube, straighten these out, drawing them down to the fingertips so that they are more or less side by side.

To cause the sticks to move apart you have only to relax the tension of your fingers when they will spring apart in an amazing manner. If the sticks do not fit too tightly into the gimmick you will find that you can even make them *jump out of your hand*. During these actions, the thumb comes underneath, resting on the tube and holding this in place. Place the sticks together and repeat this whole business several times. You can add to the effect by moving your hand in an erratic way, flicking it from side to side as you apparently discover the water in the glass. (You have merely to look for the secret mark.) Finally, pull the sticks out, relaxing pressure on the gimmick, which flies out of sight inside your sleeve. The glass which you have nominated is uncovered and everything which the audience sees can be most rigidly examined.

TELEVISION TIME

Here's a sucker trick and one that has an unusual plot

and an unusual theme. Furthermore, the props are very easy to make. Given the necessary cardboard, and a little artistic ability, (or maybe a friend with some artistic ability!) there is no reason why you should not have the finished piece of apparatus ready to use within the next hour.

EFFECT

A large plaque is shown painted to represent a television set with a large screen. Unfortunately reception doesn't seem to be too good, for the screen is covered with wavy interference lines, and no picture is visible. The magician explains this is what usually happens when he sits down to watch his favourite programme. The reception is so bad. What does he do? He decides to turn to another channel. Here he picks up a large envelope, and slides the television plaque inside it. The magician says that the picture will change and when he pulls the card out from the envelope, it indeed has changed. Now the screen is covered with *stars and squiggles*. There is still no picture to be seen! The audience are no way fooled by this deception, for the envelope has obviously been turned over and the set withdrawn the opposite way around. However, acting as though he has just presented the world's greatest mystery, the magician repeats the swindle. Again placing the plaque into the envelope, again turning the whole thing over, and pulling the card out to show the television screen is now covered with lines once more. 'Show us the other side,' the audience demand and after some byplay in which he pretends not to understand, the card *is* turned over. What is on the other side? No! *not* the expected stars and squiggles, but a notice announcing 'NORMAL SERVICE WILL BE RESUMED AS SOON AS POSSIBLE!' A great surprise finish. Finally, the envelope is torn open and then into pieces to show it is empty.

HERE'S HOW

Please don't be put off by the simplicity of the method used, for here our friend the sheath card is used again to advantage. The illustration (1) shows the construction of the sheath card, made from two pieces of 'eight sheet board', size 8 in x 10 in. The two pieces of board are Sellotaped at the edges so that they form a tube open at the two narrow

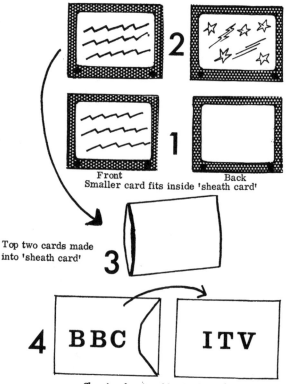

Front   Back
Smaller card fits inside 'sheath card'

Top two cards made
into 'sheath card'

Showing front and back of envelope

ends. The boards are placed together and Sellotaped at join, then folded over so the Sellotape comes on the inside. Another piece of tape is applied to the other long edge, so that it is halfway lapping the edge of the board. Tape is then folded over and two cards are pressed together. This is the same procedure as making the sheath card for the Magic Pencil trick (p 43). The advantage of this method of making the card is that all traces of preparation are actually *inside* the card and out of sight. Having made the card, paint or draw on one side, a television screen, making the card itself the actual television set! The illustration clearly shows this. A few black wavy lines on the screen represent bad reception.

The other side of the card is lettered NORMAL SERVICE WILL BE RESUMED AS SOON AS POSSIBLE or whatever notice is displayed in your country upon a breakdown in transmission. eg, 'We must apologise for the breakdown—transmission will continue soon!' There is a second card, trimmed so that it will slide into the sheath card. Again this is made from a piece of 'eight sheet board'. On one side a television set is drawn to duplicate the one on the sheath showing the wavy lines, and the reverse side shows the set with dots, spots, stars, and squiggles, again representing bad reception. The illustration (3) shows how this card will slide into the assembled sheaf, and (4) shows the final requisite, which is a large opaque envelope to take the card. Here I have the envelope lettered on one side BBC (British Broadcasting Corporation) and on the other side ITV (Independent Television). In fact the lettering on the envelope is quite optional, but does help to point the turning over of the envelope during the routine.

The working. It is simplicity itself. At the start of the trick, both the sheath card and the inner card are together but separate inside the envelope. Pick up the envelope, pulling out the small card only. Show this, place it back into the envelope, turn the envelope over and pull it out showing that the change has occurred. Repeat this, always pulling out the small card to show one side or the other. After finally showing the stars and squiggles to the audience, slide the small card into the envelope *and into the sheath card*. Finger and thumb can enter the envelope, opening the sheath slightly to make the insertion of the small card easy. Push this into the envelope, making sure the card goes snugly inside the sheath. Again turn the envelope over and now pull out the sheath card (containing the smaller card) with the wavy line side towards the audience. After some sucker byplay, turn this card over to show the wording on the back, finally tearing up the envelope to confound those who imagine you are using two cards for performing the trick. Well presented, this is an entertaining little trick and has the additional merits of being very easy to carry and very easy to perform. I hope you like it.

FINAL FORECAST

People are always interested in 'winning results' on the football pools (represented here by 'X', '1' and '2') and for audiences not football conscious the trick is just as effective with ABC folders; in fact I have myself presented it in this manner several times. We will describe it with the 'football effect', and you will see it can easily be adapted to your individual requirements.

EFFECT
The performer writes a prediction on a card, slip of paper, blackboard, or slate. Paper or card is folded and handed to a spectator. If a blackboard or slate is used it is simply placed in full view of the audience, writing side away from

them. Next, three neat little folders are displayed singly to the audience. Inside each folder is a different football symbol, '1', representing a home win, '2' standing for an away win, and finally 'X' for a draw.

The magician offers a spectator a chance of selecting the winning symbol. The three folders are shuffled around like cards and placed along in a line, on a stand, or one each into three tumblers. No one, not even the performer, knows the position of any of the symbols.

The spectator makes his choice and when the folder is opened it is seen that the magician has correctly predicted this symbol.

APPARATUS REQUIRED

If you could examine the apparatus you would find the following: one unprepared folder with an 'X' inside it, one prepared double folder which can be opened to show either a '1' or an 'X', and one prepared double folder which can be opened to show either a '2' or an 'X'.

Figure X

Figure 1

The illustration will show how the folders are constructed from card and coloured adhesive tapes. The size of each folder is $2\frac{3}{4}$ in x $4\frac{1}{4}$ in and they are boldly printed or lettered in black. The folders we use are bound with red and each has a black question mark on the cover, so they add a little eye-appeal to the stunt.

Two of the folders are really constructed from three pieces of card, the remaining one being unfeked. You will find that if all the pieces of card are the same size there will be a tendency for the centre flap to come slightly lower than the rear cover, and this is a definite help in making for easy opening of the folders at the required position. Elastic bands can be snapped around the folders if desired (useful when working close up), but these are not necessary for general use.

Folders can be nicely displayed along an ordinary card stand, or three large tumblers make ideal holders and have the advantage of appearing ordinary.

Working and routine. The working is extremely simple. The folders are opened and shown to be different, the front panel only of folder being lowered down. (If both front panels are lowered any card will show an 'X'.) You predict a 'draw' on the card or slate. After being shown, the folders are mixed up and placed along in a line, the spectator freely choosing any folder. If he chooses the unfeked one this is lifted up and given to him to open. If he chooses either of the feked ones you open it yourself, dropping both the panels together to show that your prediction was correct.

Patter. Your patter can be conversational or to suit your own style. I suggest something on the following lines.

'Everyone has dreamt of winning the football pools at some time or other, and maybe, in our imaginations we've even spent that elusive £75,000. Often we're let down by a wrong result. How nice it would be if we could see into the future and predict the correct result of a match!

'Tonight I have a premonition that someone here is in a lucky mood—it could be you, or you, or you! Perhaps sir, it's YOUR lucky night. Would you help me from where you are sitting?

'I'll put down here, for the record, the result of a match. Let's imagine for the moment it's a match between............ and............ (name two local teams). Not quite in the first division but they will serve for this test. There are three possible results. A home win, an away win, or a draw —represented by these three symbols most of you know so well. I'll mix them up and place them along like this. You have a perfectly free choice of any one of these—and don't forget—tonight is your lucky night! Which is it to be? Would you like to change your mind? Right. It's a draw— and the correct result of the match—a draw! Marvellous! A pair of draws . . . sorry! Don't forget this is your lucky night, so when you go home, fill in your coupon and if you DO win . . . don't forget to thank me! Write your thanks on the back of a FIVE POUND NOTE! I'd appreciate it as much as you have appreciated our little demonstration this evening.'

I hope you'll like this little trick and get a great deal of pleasure from its performance.

TRAVELLING TRANSISTOR

With transistor radios used so much these days, you can't go wrong with this effect.

EFFECT

A transistor radio is displayed and the performer switches

in on so the audience can hear the latest pop records which are being transmitted.

An opera hat is placed upside down on the table, and a china plate is placed on top, covering the opening completely. On this is placed the radio, still playing merrily, then a cover that just fits over it.

'Watch,' says the magician as he quickly lifts up the cover to show that the radio has vanished and penetrated the plate to appear inside the hat.

APPARATUS REQUIRED

For this you require a box-type transistor radio and a duplicate shell which fits over the genuine article. The shell can be made from cardboard and is fitted with spare front parts which can be bought from the radio shop. The cover used is also made of cardboard, and fits tightly over the shell so that, when it is inside it can be shown empty. The shell radio has no base, so it is possible to show the cover to be empty.

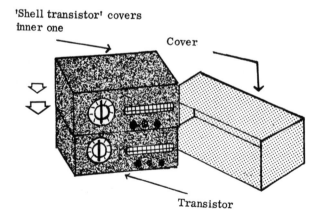

'Shell transistor' covers inner one

Cover

Transistor

The set-up is easy, for at the start the shell is inside the cover and the radio is on the table. An opera hat and plate are also close by ready for the presentation of the effect.

Working and Presentation. The radio is picked up, displayed, and switched on so the audience can hear it. It is covered with the cover for a second whilst the performer explains exactly what he intends doing. Lifted up again, the cover is removed and the shell is loaded over the genuine transistor. The hat is shown empty at this stage and the transistor (with shell) is placed inside, and the magician explains that this is the easy way of making the radio appear inside the hat; but he intends showing the audience the magical way. At this stage, he places the china plate over the mouth of the hat. With the radio still playing, the audience thinks, of course, that it comes from the shell, which looks identical. The shell radio is placed on top of the plate and the cover is placed over this. The audience can still clearly hear the radio even when the cover is dramatically lifted away to reveal that it has vanished.

The plate is shown to be quite solid and there beneath it is the transistor, which is immediately lifted out and handed round for examination if wished. The hat is shown empty too, for this has truly been a wonderful penetration.

EGG AND CONFETTI

A pretty effect for your platform shows. The magician shows a beaker together with a box of confetti. He fills the beaker with confetti, then tips it back into the box. He fills the beaker again, now, however, covering it with a handkerchief and giving it to someone to hold. At any time he can lift the handkerchief to show that the beaker is really filled with confetti.

From the spectator's nose the magician produces an egg.

He places the egg in his hand, but the egg vanishes and appears from behind his knee. Once more the egg is placed in his hand and now the magician takes up a fan. He fans his hand and from it emerges a shower of confetti—the egg has gone! He uncovers the beaker, there inside it is the egg. Finally, to bring the effect to its conclusion, he cracks this into the beaker, proving it to be the real thing.

HERE'S HOW

The method is really very simple. You use a real egg for the climax. This is in a beaker and on top of this goes a disc of cardboard. To the top of this disc has been glued some confetti; a piece of thread has been attached to the disc and hangs over the top of the beaker; a bead is fastened to the thread.

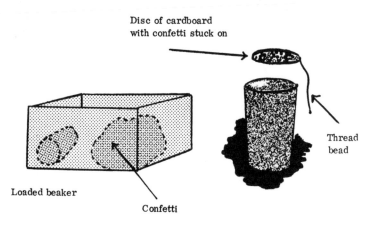

Disc of cardboard
with confetti stuck on

Thread
bead

Loaded beaker

Confetti

At the start, this beaker is in the box of confetti.

The other egg is prepared. Take an ordinary egg, make a hole in each end of it, and blow out the contents. Now dry the egg thoroughly in the oven, and when it is dry, carefully fill it with confetti. The end holes are plugged up, either with gummed paper or with sealing wax. The egg now resembles the real thing.

At the start, this is on the table behind the box of confetti.

PRESENTATION

Show a duplicate, empty beaker, Scoop this full with confetti, pouring the confetti back into the box. You can repeat this several times. Finally, come out of the box with the beaker which really holds the egg, and which has the 'feke' disc on the top of it. You can tilt the beaker over and the audience can see that the beaker appears to be filled with confetti. The beaker is covered over and given to a spectator to hold. As you place the box of confetti to one side, 'steal' the egg from behind it, and perform a few moves with this as per the sleight of hand section in this book—producing the egg from a spectator's nose, vanishing it, and so on. Finally place the egg in the left hand. The right hand picks up a fan. Crush the egg, at the same time releasing the confetti and fanning this so that it flies all over the place. Allow the pieces of dried egg to fall with the confetti. Now go over to the spectator who is holding the beaker. Grasp the bead through the handkerchief, make sure that the spectator is holding the beaker firmly or take it from him yourself, and lift the handkerchief, taking the disc away underneath it. Pocket the handkerchief or place it to one side.

Now from the beaker you tip the egg, showing that this is otherwise empty. Finally, crack the egg into the beaker to bring an interesting magical sequence to its conclusion.

This little routine is of real professional calibre and yet the apparatus is so very, very simple to acquire, the cost being only a few shillings or cents.

MAGICAL PRINTING

This next effect looks like real magic, yet the properties used are simple and easily obtainable.

The performer displays a pack of cards which, he states, has not been fully printed. The back designs are on the cards but the faces are plain. The cards are fanned and it is seen that the faces are indeed plain. The magician squares the cards together, and then refans them, showing that it is now a regular pack, every card being fully printed!

HERE'S HOW

You require a normal pack of cards. The secret lies in the special extra card required and this can easily be made by using the Joker from the same pack. Cover this with 'Fablon', 'Contact', or similar material, or a white paper would be adequate. In other words this one card is a blank-faced one and this should be on the front of the pack. Have the pack in its case. Take the cards out squarely and hold them in the left hand. As our illustration shows,

Fanned up to show
blanks

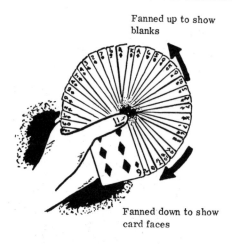

Fanned down to show
card faces

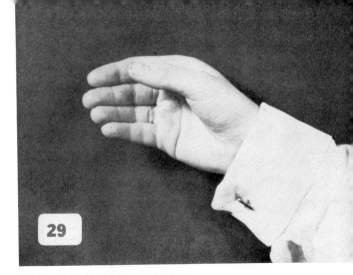

29

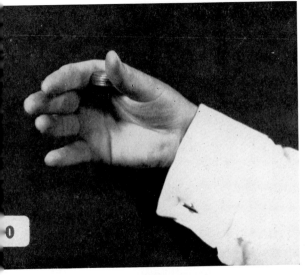

0

Page 89: Catching coins in the air (29) *Front view showing hand to be empty;* (30) *exposure of coins being concealed between thumb and index finger;* (31) *plan view showing stack of coins held ready for producing*

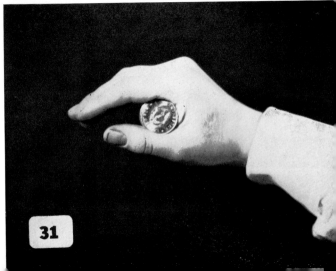

31

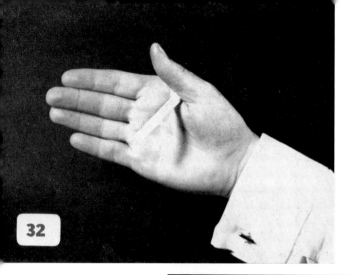

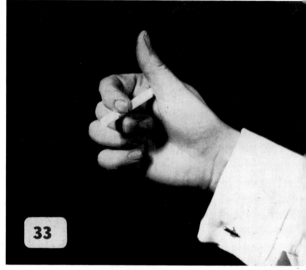

Page 90: A cigarette vanish or production (32) *Rear view showing cigarette 'thumb palmed';* (33) *fingers curl inwards to pick up cigarette;* (34) *two fingers extend to produce it from concealed position*

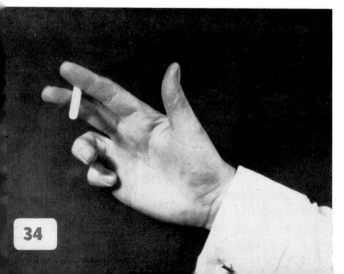

the pack can be 'reverse fanned', a term magicians give to a pack being fanned out anti-clockwise instead of clockwise (the natural way of fanning cards). By fanning in this way the pack looks absolutely blank, for the edges of the cards (which do not have indices on this side) show as plain and white. The added blank card on the front gives the illusion that these are all plain cards. The fan of cards is closed up, the magician turning the pack over and refanning them towards himself.

'My friend is a printer,' explains the magician 'but he has forgotten to print the faces of this pack. Well, every man to his own trade. I'm a magician, and to prove it, how's that.' As the performer makes these remarks the pack is turned over and seen to be printed. Our illustration shows that the pack can now be fanned in a clockwise fashion and the performer does this with the faces facing him at the present moment. The blank card still remains to the front, but this is removed, and shown, as he recaps the fact that all the cards are blank. Showing this single card adds to the illusion that all the cards are plain. He replaces this, *but to the rear of the fan,* out of sight. By simply reversing the pack, the printed faces can be seen. Presented slickly the effect is over before the audience get a chance to think just how the change was made.

4

Simple Sleight of Hand

I F YOU were to ask a layman what sleight of hand in magic consists of, he would probably say 'palming', and to a degree he would be right. It is a word often used by magicians, and although this method has been widely exposed it still forms the basis of much sleight-of-hand work. Palming enables you secretly to hold an article in the hand but in a natural position, without the audience suspecting that there is anything there.

It is possible in these pages to give you only the basic techniques of sleight-of-hand moves which make some brilliant magical effects possible and create the overall image of skill.

If you can vanish a coin, a ball, or similar object, you will find that you can vanish almost anything of similar size —a key, a pen, or a watch. Once you have learnt the basic moves, it is an easy matter to vanish or produce any object in the hands. This to many magicians is real magic, but to me, as an all-round magician who likes to vary his magic, it is just another branch of this fascinating art of ours.

We are going to learn how to vanish small objects in

the hands, how to produce them, and how to change them from one thing into another of a completely different nature. From here our talents can go to making objects pass from one hand to the other, making them change colour, and all these effects are performed without specially made apparatus.

In this simple guide to sleight of hand I have tried to take the reader on a short cut, avoiding the very many clever-clever moves which have to be practised for years.

Although simple moves are explained, these serve the same purpose as the more elaborate ones, enabling you to achieve the same magical effects. In most of the effects you appear to transfer an article from one hand (let us assume the right one) into the other. In actual fact the article is retained in the right hand and is concealed there in a natural manner. *This* is where palming comes in.

It is possible to grip the concealed article in the palm position by flexing the hand around it, or, in many instances, two fingers can be curled inwards to hold the article. *Always aim at naturalness in performance.*

Remember that misdirection too is so important.

When you have an article in the right hand and you have 'transferred it into the left' (really retaining it in the right), *look* at the left hand as though the article was really there. Point to the left hand with the right one and appear surprised when you open the left hand to find the article which you supposedly placed there has vanished into thin air.

A SIMPLE BILLIARD BALL MOVE

Let us assume that you wish to vanish a billiard ball (the same move can be applied to the vanish of any small article or object, a cube of sugar perhaps, a ball of wool, a pocket watch). This move is often performed with a coin and is known as the 'French Drop'. The photographs I have taken show a billiard ball, so a billiard ball it is.

The photographs on pp 35-6 show the performer's view. The first shows a billiard ball held in the right hand.

In the second, the left hand comes over as though to take it. The fingers partially close round the ball in the third photograph. However, the ball is allowed to drop down into the palm of the right hand as in the third and fourth photographs.

The fifth shows how three fingers of the right hand curl inwards to hold the ball securely. The hand turns over so that its back is fully towards the audience. The right hand points to the left hand which has been closed as though containing the ball. The seventh photograph shows the audience's view at this stage.

Now slowly and dramatically, with a sort of 'crumpling movement' of the fingers open out the left hand, at the same time turning this over to show that the ball has vanished.

THE BALL REAPPEARS

The right hand can now reach behind the knee or it can make a grabbing movement into the air. The concealed ball in the right hand is brought up into view.

If you will study the photographs you will see how very easy this move is.

Whether you are a close-up performer or a stage magician, it is always a good thing to know how to vanish small articles or objects. Audiences appreciate seeing clever tricks with the hands. Even if you are presenting big stage illusions an interlude of sleight of hand is acceptable between the larger illusions, enabling these to be 'set' behind the curtains.

ANOTHER VANISH

Again this uses a billiard ball and again the move is quite adaptable. You can vanish a tomato in this way or almost any small article. The right hand is formed into a fist and the article which is to be vanished is placed on the top of it as in the first photograph on p 18.

The second shows how the left hand now comes forward and closes around the article as though to take it away. What really happens is that the right fist is relaxed so that the article goes down inside the fist. The left hand closes around the imaginary article and is drawn away as in the third and fourth photographs.

The fifth photograph on p 18 shows the true state of affairs and how the ball, or what-have-you, is really kept in the right hand concealed by the fingers.

If you like you can now vanish the ball which you are supposed to have in the left hand by 'throwing this into the air', making the throwing movement with the left hand, following the supposed flight of the ball upwards with your eyes. You would be surprised how often members of the audience will swear that they saw the ball vanish in mid-air! The ball or other missing object is reproduced by the right hand.

TAKE-AWAY VANISH

This is an extremely easy move to execute. We have shown it as being performed with a coin, but the move is adaptable to any article which can be gripped in the fingers. The coin is placed on the right hand where it is really gripped with the palm, ie the fleshy part of the root of the thumb and the actual palm of the hand. The left hand comes over to take the coin and as the fingers supposedly close around it so the right hand turns over so that its back is towards the audience as shown in the second and third photographs on p 53. The fourth shows the hand can casually rest on the left hand which now dramatically opens to show that the coin has vanished.

A ROUND-ABOUT VANISH

This is an extremely easy vanish to perform and one which is very adaptable. I know of several magicians who use this move in preference to all others. It can be used for vanishing a thimble, a coin, or any small article. The left hand is formed into a fist; it is held loosely as in the first photograph on p 54. The right hand takes any small article (in this instance a coin), and pushes it partially into the fist. Now the right thumb continues this pushing-in movement, the right hand fingers coming underneath the left fist. The fingers of the left hand are held fairly loosely and as the coin or what-have-you is pressed completely into the hand as the third photograph on p 54 so it is allowed to pass through the fingers and back into the right hand where it is gripped as shown in the fourth photograph.

A SIMPLE PALM

Early in this chapter I mentioned palming and in the strict classical sense this means holding an object in the hand with the fingers extended. However, as I previously mentioned in this chapter and as is clearly shown in the photographs on p 71 it is not necessary always to have the fingers extended. The first photograph shows the audience's view of the hand held in a very natural position and used to point to an article or to the other hand, whereas in fact, as the second photograph shows, a ball is concealed there. The hand can reach up into the air, pushing down with the the thumb and out on the ball to bring this to the tips of the fingers.

PRODUCING A THIMBLE

Here is a useful little flourish which again teaches you magic, and you will find that you can use this method to produce other items as well as thimbles. For example, if you have a billiard ball with a hole in it you can do all sorts of marvellous little stunts similar to this one. In this instance an ordinary thimble is used and the first photograph on p 72 shows how the magician brings both his hands up together, palms towards the audience, to show them empty. The second photograph shows that there is really a thimble on the right thumb but this is behind the left hand unseen.

The hands are swung around now, the thumb moves down behind the right hand, which partially closes round it and the forefinger points to the left hand as though something was going to make its appearance from there. Then swing around, pointing now to the right hand and suddenly pop the thimble on the thumb up into view. A surprising appearance!

Do not always use the same move all the time but vary your method of vanishing and also vary the methods of actually producing articles, sometimes producing them from the body, sometimes from the air, from a person's nose, and so on. In other words, try to add as much *variety* as possible to your performance.

You will see that using the simple basic moves I have given you, you will be able to produce a thimble, vanish it, produce it again and so on, or a similar sequence can be carried through using billiard balls or coins.

CATCHING COINS IN THE AIR

The popular trick entitled 'The Miser's Dream' can be a hit in any magician's programme. The magician shows his hands to be empty, then reaches up in the air and produces a coin. One after the other a succession of coins appear.

Page 89 shows a method of concealing a whole stack of coins. Of course the hands must be angled correctly but you will be surprised how deceptive this method of holding coins is.

To produce them, bend back the forefinger and second finger, sliding a coin off from the top of the stack and bringing this into view at the fingertips. Repeat this procedure with the other coins one at a time until all have made their appearance.

A CIGARETTE VANISH OR PRODUCTION

Let us assume you wish to vanish a cigarette. The third photograph on p 90 shows how this is held between the forefinger and second finger in the usual smoking position. Now as the hand is waved in the air the fingers bend inwards as in the second photograph. Finally, the cigarette is gripped at the crutch of the thumb as shown in the first photograph. This is what is known in magic as the 'thumb palm' position. If you will reverse the order of the sequence, that is start off at Photograph 32, then bring the fingers in as in 33, reaching out as in 34 to show the cigarette there, you will appear to have magically produced a cigarette from the air.

98

A COMPLETE ROUTINE
PRODUCING TWELVE CIGARETTES FROM
THE AIR

The effect of producing cigarettes from the air is a classic one and one which never fails to evoke the admiration of an audience. The routine which I give you here is quite easy to learn and to perform. However, *practice* is essential in order that you should perform the sequence *cleanly and smoothly,* without any fumbling. One should practise in front of a mirror before setting out to perform the effect in public.

The routine commences when the performer displays a flat opera hat, springing this open. If preferred, an ordinary hat can be used in its place. An opera hat (and you will find that you can often obtain these from secondhand clothes shops) looks professional and certainly adds to the effect.

The magician removes a single cigarette from a packet. He sniffs it, doesn't appear to like it, and places it in the hat. He reaches out into the air and a second cigarette apears; this is placed in the hat.

The empty hand again reaches high into the air producing cigarette number three.

Another cigarette is produced from behind the knee and so on until *twelve* in all have been magically materialised! Finally all the cigarettes are tipped from the hat, showing the audience the concluding result of your conjuring skill!

All you need for this trick are thirteen cigarettes (preferably tipped variety), one opera hat (or any other kind of hat if you are unable to obtain one of these), and an empty cigarette packet.

SET UP

Place two of the cigarettes inside the packet with the tipped ends upwards, then close the lid. Place the packet in your right jacket pocket. If you are using an opera hat, spring this open, placing the remaining eleven cigarettes in the bottom of it, then carefully closing the hat flat so that the cigarettes are trapped under its springs. When the hat is sprung open the cigarettes will be inside it.

If a trilby or bowler hat is used, place the cigarettes around the inside hat rim, which is usually made of leather and wide enough to hold the load without its being seen. It is unnecessary to make a big fuss about displaying the hat; simply pick it up crown uppermost, then turn it over with its mouth upwards, and go into the routine.

WORKING

Show the hat, or spring it open in the case of the opera hat, and place it on the table.

Photograph 35 shows how the cigarettes are concealed under the springs of the hat, and 36 shows the open hat. See p 107.

The right hand goes to the pocket, removing the cigarette packet from there. The packet is transferred into the left hand. The top of the packet is opened. The right hand goes to the packet to remove a cigarette and as this occurs the second cigarette is gripped and retained in the thumb-palm position (see last two photographs on p 107). The packet is immediately discarded. To the audience you have merely removed a cigarette. Place the cigarette between your lips, then remove it again, looking at the brand and so on, before tossing it into the hat. Straight away reach up into the air with the right hand, carrying out the production method as detailed and illustrated in photographs on p 90, and bring the second cigarette into view. This cigarette is now apparently placed in the hat, in reality it is brought back into the crutch of the thumb as soon as the hand enters the hat.

The hand again reaches up into the air and produces cigarette number three. This business is repeated.

Try to vary the ways in which you produce the cigarette. Produce it from behind your knee, from the air, from your elbow, and so on, placing the cigarettes in quick succession in the hat which you can now at this stage hold in your left hand, moving around the audience if you wish whilst producing the cigarettes. Finally, tip all the cigarettes out into a bowl, and distribute them to the audience.

Alternative Finish. By having the hat actually empty all the way through you can tilt the hat over at the end to show that all the cigarettes have vanished. A better finish is to have a few cigars inside the hat, showing that the cigarettes have magically changed into cigars!

Your Final Smoke. A novel finish is to place the last cigarette between your lips, and, reaching behind the lapel of your jacket, you produce a lit match which you use to light the cigarette! After the cigarette has been lit the burning match is held in the right hand. Blow down your left hand jacket sleeve when suddenly and magically the match goes out!

Special Gimmick. There is a special little gadget used for the production of the lit match. This is very easily made from the two striking surfaces from a box of safety matches. These two strips are cut off and placed together, an elastic band being placed around them. A safety pin holds this little gadget in position under the lapel. Between this sandwich of striking surfaces are placed a couple of safety matches. You will find that when you withdraw a match this is automatically lit. If you are using matches of the non-safety

101

variety, two strips of sandpaper stuck on to cardboard do the same trick.

Blow-out Match. This is a cute little flourish and easy to perform. As you hold the lit match in your outstretched right hand, blow down your left sleeve and the match goes out. Unknown to the audience you quickly snap the bottom of the match with your thumb, which flicks the flame out. You will have to practise this, but you will find it is quite easy to do and most effective. Again misdirection is used for whilst the audience's eyes are following you blowing down your left sleeve your right hand is really at work.

MYSTERIOUS PAPER BALLS

Here is a trick which you can perform with a variety of articles—sponge balls, sugar lumps, pom-poms, and so on. In this instance it is performed with some sheets of tissue paper. Many things happen during the routine.

Three sheets of tissue paper are crumpled up into three paper balls. The performer counts them—'one, two, three'. He picks up two of the balls with the right hand and places them in the left. The third ball is shown and placed in the jacket pocket out of sight. When the left hand is opened there are still one, two, *three* balls inside it! 'I will do that again,' says the magician. Again a ball is taken away and placed in the pocket but again it appears to jump from there, for when the left hand is opened the *three* balls of paper are seen there.

Now the magician goes a step further, picking up two of the paper balls and giving these to a spectator to hold. The third ball is displayed and vanished in the hand. When the spectator opens his hand up he now has three balls of paper there.

The three balls are crumpled together as one and the

magician throws these towards the spectator, asking him to open them out. When he does so there is a big surprise, for the three pieces of paper have now merged into one large piece displaying the boldly lettered words 'KEEP LITTER OFF THE STREETS'.

REQUIREMENTS

The only thing used is tissue paper! The large extra piece is lettered with a felt marker pen and used for the climax. In addition to this, you use three small pieces and, the item the audience knows nothing of, an extra ball of tissue paper. This extra ball of paper is in fact concealed during the whole routine and it can be retained by the thumb palm or held with the curled-in two fingers of the hand as the reader desires. It makes no difference and it is advisable to use the method which you yourself favour.

I suggest that at the start this extra ball of paper be concealed just under the edge of the jacket. It can be held there with an ordinary hairgrip secured in place by a safety pin.

In performance show your hands empty, having the three pieces of tissue paper in front of you. The large crumpled up ball of paper is in the right-hand jacket pocket.

Crumple up each of the pieces of paper in turn so that you have the three balls of paper. Stand back from the table momentarily to emphasise this, the right hand meanwhile getting hold of the extra ball of paper from under the edge of the jacket and concealing it. Pick up one of the balls of paper from the table, placing this in the left-hand fingers. Pick up the second ball of paper in the right hand, placing this along with the first ball in the left-hand fingers. *However, this time the ball of paper which you have concealed in the right hand is added to it so the left hand now holds the three balls of paper.*

Pick up the remaining ball of paper on the table with the right hand, placing it into the right-hand jacket pocket. Immediately this is kept concealed in the right hand, in the thumb palm or, as previously stated, in the natural curve of the fingers.

Meanwhile the left hand has 'opened out', the three pieces of paper being dropped on to the table. The ball of paper has magically returned there!

Repeat this process with the balls of paper on the table. Pick up the first ball of paper, placing it in the right hand. This time add the concealed ball. Say 'Oh yes, the ball of paper is still there.' Open the left hand squeezing the two balls of paper together as one and showing the 'ball of paper' there. The right hand now picks up the second ball of paper from the table, placing this also in the left hand. The third ball is picked up and placed into the pocket, again being secretly concealed in the hand as previously.

The left hand opens and the three balls of paper drop out.

Pick up two balls of paper, one in each hand, and place these together in the right hand, concealing the concealed ball with them. Ask a spectator to hold the 'two balls of paper' tightly. (Unknown to him he now holds three of these.)

Take up and put the remaining ball of paper on the table, vanishing this by any of the moves which I have given. I suggest that you use the one where the left hand is formed into a loose fist, the right hand fingers and thumb pushing the ball of paper in and around the left thumb and back into the right hand.

The spectator is asked to open his hand. To his surprise he has the three paper balls there.

The magician places these once more on the table in front of him. He places one in his left hand, another one in his left hand, then picks up the remaining ball from the table and puts it into his pocket. As soon as his hand is there, inside the pocket, he drops the concealed ball, and picks up the large wad of papers concealed there. The hand emerges from the pocket, still containing the one ball apparently. The left hand is opened to show that there are still two balls there.

The three balls of paper are wadded together with the large ball of paper; everything is held together as one. The left hand comes over, taking away the large ball only. The three single balls are kept concealed in the right hand. The wad of papers is tossed to a spectator, and under cover of this the right hand draws back, depositing the three balls in the pocket.

The spectator is asked to open out the papers and see how many he has there. One, two, or three? No, only the *one* paper, the large one bearing the tag line which brings a laugh and this clever routine to a pleasant close.

POTS OF PLENTY

Magicians familiar with the old tricks of yesteryear will know that the following effect is that of really ancient mystery, but in this case brought up-to-date.

This routine has never previously appeared in any book or publication devoted to magic or magicians. It is new, and specially devised for this book. Much care has been taken to create the same mystery as in the old 'Cups and Balls', as the trick is widely known.

The trick has been presented for thousands of years, and in every country. It was presented in Victorian drawing-rooms, it was and still is performed on the streets of India where passers-by can witness magic being presented close up, and it still appears on stage and on television.

In France it is called 'le Jeu des Gobelets' and every conjurer worthy of his salt is expected to be able to perform the effect. From country to country magicians have used different types of goblets or beakers but still the effect remained the same. This is the miraculous effect of balls appearing, vanishing, and penetrating the three examined cups which are used throughout the routine.

Some magical writers have stated that one must only use the accepted, standard set of metal cups which are specially manufactured for the purpose, otherwise the effect is not 'pure magic'. How wrong they are!

The late Johnny Ramsay from Ayr, Scotland, earned a fantastic reputation by presenting this famous trick with ice cream cartons. The fact that he was using commonplace articles such as these added to the mystery. When his routine was over, he would pass out the cups and let the spectators keep them, a climax which, to my mind, was more telling than that of the performer who carefully gathered up his specially chrome-plated cups for his next performance! Occasionally, and for stage use, I too like using the set of special plated goblets for the cups and balls, and amongst my collection is a set which was presented to me by the late Burtini, an expert manufacturer of the correct cups for the trick. These are accepted as tools of the trade and have their place in magic. However, the routine I explain here differs from others.

Here we use no special plated cups costing several guineas. Instead we have a gardening theme, and use gardening pots. Instead of sponge balls, we finish with flowerheads. The magic wand normally used throughout the routine has gone also and we use a 'labelling stick' as used in gardening. *The entire outfit costs as little as one shilling to buy from your local gardening store.*

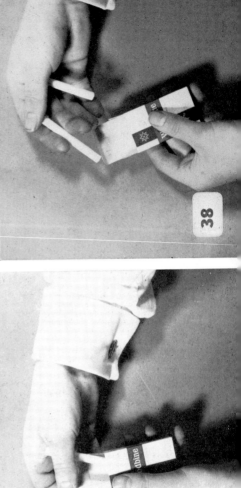

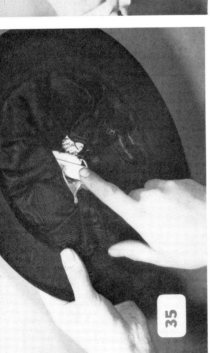

Page 107: Producing twelve cigarettes from the air (35) Folded opera hat containing secreted cigarettes beneath lining; (36) hat sprung open. Cigarettes drop inside; (37) remove cigarette from packet. Second cigarette being 'thumb palmed'; (38) cigarette now removed, duplicate now firmly gripped in same position

39

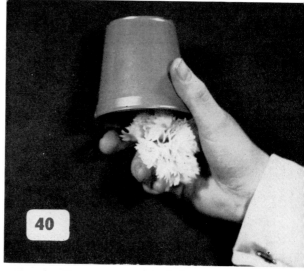

40

Page 108 : Pots of plenty (39) *The proper-ties as seen by the audience;* (40) *loading of the flower-head. Flower held in palm position;* (41) *pot is lowered, flower drops inside*

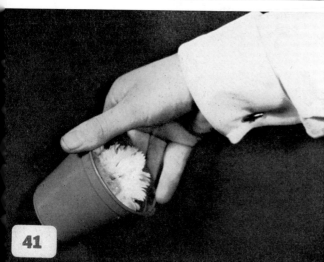

41

APPARATUS REQUIRED

Three plastic pots as used for gardening purposes.

Four sponge circles cut from nylon foam sponge. These represent 'seeds' during the sequence.

Three tops cut from plastic carnations.

One labelling stick which can be bought in packets of six or a dozen.

SET UP

Have the three carnation tops in your left-hand jacket pocket out of view. Three of the sponge discs are in your right-hand jacket pocket.

The cups are nested together and you will find that there is a space between the nested cups enabling you to conceal any of the discs there.

The fourth, unsuspected, disc is secretly dropped into one of the cups, the other two being nested inside it. The nest of cups should rest on your table, mouth upwards, with the labelling stick beside it.

PERFORMANCE

The cups are turned mouth downwards on the table, the secret disc now lying on top of the centre cup. The stack of cups is lifted and flashed inside and then the performer begins to place the cups mouth downwards upon the table one at a time. In doing this, 'The Gallop', as magicians call it, is executed. This is the term given to the cups being swung over one at a time on to the table mouth downwards, without letting the hidden disc drop out. It simply goes over with the cup and no one is the wiser. It is much like the old stunt of swinging a bucket of water round and round without letting the water come out, the disc being held by centrifugal force. When the cups are placed along in the

109

row from right to left, the hidden ball should be under the right-hand cup. The performer goes to his pocket and removes the first disc and holds it in his right hand. He pretends to place it in his left but secretly retains it in the right. The French Drop (p 94), previously described for the vanish of objects, will be suitable for this move and you must refer to the details and action photographs (p 108).

The left hand appears to hold the ball and the right hand, still concealing the disc, lifts up the left-hand cup slightly at an angle to the front, and the left hand pretends to slip the ball under this cup. The fact that the hand is empty now proves that it must have been put there. The magician points with his right hand at the cup, and commands the disc to jump from the left-hand cup to the right. He lifts up the right-hand cup with the right hand revealing the disc there.

Whilst the audience's eyes are on the disc which has just appeared, the right hand allows the disc it holds to drop into the cup. PHOTOGRAPHS 40 and 41 show the move clearly but with a flower head. The procedure is exactly the same with the disc. The cup is held in an upward position and then dropped down, the disc being allowed to fall inside.

Take away the disc which has just appeared under this cup, and replace the cup, doing the gallop move again. Now the secret disc is in the same position, under the right-hand cup. This time the performer states that he will make the disc pass from his hand and appear under any cup the spectator wishes.

The disc is placed in the left hand, but secretly retained in the right. The closed left hand is quickly opened to show the disc has gone. If the spectator wishes the disc to appear under the left-hand cup, this hand goes to the cup, slowly lifts it up, at the same time dropping the disc. The illusion is created that the disc came from under the cup.

If the spectator's choice was the centre cup, the same move is applied. If the choice was for the right-hand cup, the disc does not have to be loaded under the cup, for there is one there all the time.

In the event of the right-hand cup being chosen, when the disc is removed from the cup, the secret one is loaded inside again so that there is still a disc under the right-hand cup.

Now comes a penetration. The secret disc is under the right cup. The disc in view is placed on top of this cup. The performer states that there are small holes on top of the pot, and he will make the disc pass through these. An impossible sounding feat. The centre cup is placed on top of the right-hand cup and finally the third on top of the others. This last one is slammed down rather dramatically, and the *whole stack* is lifted to show that the disc is now at the bottom, having penetrated through the others!

The cups are parted and, again by the aid of the gallop move, are placed along in a row on the table, bringing the hidden disc under the centre cup. The disc in view is lifted again and vanished in the left hand (by any of the vanishes described throughout the pages of this book). The right hand lifts up the centre cup and there the disc is beneath it!

When replacing this cup over the disc, the second disc is loaded in as previously described, now leaving *two* underneath.

Performer goes to his right-hand pocket and removes another disc and vanishes this in a similar manner. The labelling stick can be lifted at intervals so it can be magically tapped against the hand just prior to the vanish. (It gives you a good reason to keep the hand holding it partially closed!) The centre cup is lifted and the two discs are revealed.

When being replaced over these two the third disc is

secretly loaded. The next disc in the pocket is removed and vanished until there are the three discs together—under the cups.

At this stage a disc (the fourth one) is secretly hidden in the right hand which is quietly pocketed. The three discs which are in view are now placed on top of each of the cups and one by one they are lifted from there and placed in the left-hand pocket. In doing so the first disc is taken, and this, is placed inside the pocket, the now empty hand getting hold of one of the flower-heads in the secret palm position. The cup is lifted with the right hand whilst the left comes away from the pocket with this hidden flower-head. The cup is transferred from right hand to the left and on page 108 the loading method is clearly shown. The flower-head is allowed to drop into the cup as this is lowered downwards, and the cup is quickly dropped upon the table now containing this.

The second disc is placed in the pocket and again a flower-head is secretly withdrawn and loaded.

The third and last disc is removed from the top of its cup and in a similar fashion to the others is placed in the pocket. Again you secretly bring out a flower-head in the palm position and again load this.

At this stage three flower-heads are inside each cup.

So far the audience has seen the performer remove the discs one by one and place them in the pocket. What they are next expecting does not really happen. They really visualise the discs returning to their correct places under the cups. But in actual fact, when individually lifted, each cup reveals a nice flower-head, each of a different colour, underneath!

The entire apparatus—cups, flower-heads, labelling stick —can be thoroughly examined, for no feked apparatus has been used. It is all done by sleight of hand!

The 'Cups and Balls' trick will live on for many years, long after we depart from this world, and that is why I wish the reader of this book to present this miracle, but in a different style and with a different theme. Different as it may be, you will still be credited for clever manipulations and with presenting good magic.

MARVELLOUS MONEY BOX

Already I have detailed a complete cigarette production using a simple sleight-of-hand method, and here I explain a sequence of productions with coins, from the air, which are then pushed through the slot of a small money box. The coins seem to appear from the air, under the arm, from the nose, and even on spectators' clothing.

KNOW-HOW

First let us take a look at the first photograph on p 125, which shows us the type of cash box required for the effect. This one is a cheap tin model costing very little and does the purpose extremely well. The fact that it is made from tin enables us to cut a slot at the rear. This slot can be cut with a tin opener, and then filed wider, so that when a coin is dropped through the slot in the top of the cash tin, it will slide out into the hand when the tin is simply tilted backwards. The second photograph shows the coins sliding into the palm of the hand. During the routine it is also possible to hold the box by the handle as the lid will firmly hold in this position without locking the box.

You will also require six coins, and the ones I use are brass amusement discs which polish up extremely well and give the trick more appeal, appearing as 'gold'. Furthermore, the effect can be presented in any country, for 'golden coins' appear valuable to all.

The preparation is simple. Six coins are held in the palm of the right hand at the start, unseen by the audience. The cash box is held in the left hand, with the opening towards the rear.

Reach into the air and slide off coin number one (third photograph on p 125) and drop it through the slot in the top of the box. Produce another and then a third, rattling the box as you do this. After the third comes the fourth, and when this is placed inside, the three coins already inside the box are allowed to slide out into the hand. This will never be seen, for the box gives you complete cover. Carry on with the production of the other two coins, dropping them inside as before. When your right hand is empty, transfer the box from left to right, retaining the three coins, which are now in the left hand. The right hand holds the box in the same manner as before. The left hand reaches into the air and produces the three coins one at a time, and during this time the coins in the box slide out through the opening at the rear and into the right hand. From here the reader will visualise what in fact happens throughout the entire sequence. The box is transferred from one hand to the other, but in the process, coins are allowed to slide out from the box into the hand. This means that a continuous stream of coins can be produced until you think sufficient have been 'caught'. I would advise the performer not to overdo the number used, for it is always better to leave the audience wanting more than in a state of surfeit. Keep the cash tin rattling, it adds to the effect.

If you wish, the coin sleight detailed on p 98 and photographs on p 89 could well be used for the production throughout.

An extra climax can be created when the performer opens the box to find no coins, but a note (pound note, dollar bill, etc), the coins having magically changed into paper money.

To do this, allow all coins to slide into the hand at the end. A folded note has been 'waxed' or lightly Sellotaped inside the lid of the box, away from the slot, or to the rear of the box.

At the climax, after the coins are allowed to glide into the hand, the box is opened and this note is unfolded and removed, the box then being shown empty.

'Marvellous money box' has been produced specially for this book, and although it is based on old principles, no other magicians at this present time are using the item, so you will have something 'exclusive'. It could well be the trick which will make you famous. Try it!

MELT THROUGH COIN

Not a trick on its own, but a neat stunt to use when presenting tricks with coins, such as the 'Marvellous money box' which I have just explained. After some coins have been produced, the performer displays one and rubs it right through the back of his hand!

Simplicity is the keynote and with a little practice this stunt will look extremely skilful.

To prepare for the item you first must conceal a duplicate coin in the left hand before the start of the trick. As this hand is in the form of a fist throughout, no palming is required.

The first photograph on p 126 shows the left hand formed into a fist (retaining coin), whilst the right holds another coin between the finger and thumb against the back of the left hand to emphasise to the audience that you are going to do something with that part of the hand. Believe me, these small details help to make the trick clear, concise, and visual.

The second photograph shows the right hand starting

to push the coin through. What in fact happens is that the right hand moves down over the coin as it moves across the back of the hand. The third photograph shows how the hand is now at the other side of the fist and the coin is no longer in view. When presented quickly and smoothly it does look as though the coin has penetrated the back of the hand.

I have often introduced this neat item into a series of coin manipulations with success.

Once the coin has passed through, the left hand immediately turns over to show the (duplicate) coin there in the palm of the hand. Notice how in the fourth photograph on p 126 the fingers of the right hand curl in even though it contains the other coin. To conclude the trick the right hand lifts up the coin off the hand and places it in the pocket together with the other palmed one.

VANISHING AND PRODUCING A CARD

Magicians all over the world are acclaimed for their skill and dexterity when using playing cards. Card manipulations *look* skilful, and indeed they are! To produce cards from the air one after the other singly or in fans, is not an easy matter, and something which cannot be learnt overnight. It is done with practice alone.

Several books, available to magicians, have been published on this one branch of magic alone.

It is my intention here to explain the basic back and front palming as used in this type of magic, so that you will be able to reach into the air and produce a card, and if you wish, vanish it again. The cards can be normal playing cards, your own, or borrowed from a friend.

Using this technique you may produce your business card, presenting it to a person you are about to introduce yourself to. He immediately knows the type of business you are in, and the production makes a novel introduction which he may always remember.

With the aid of the following photographs, you will soon grasp the action of vanishing the card.

To vanish a playing card, make sure it is between the finger and thumb as in the first photograph on p 143. The next photograph shows how the two centre fingers curl downwards, but the thumb still retains a firm grip on the front. The vital move is shown in the third photograph. As the thumb grips the card firmly, the index and little fingers clamp down on top of the card along the edges. You will now find it an easy matter to allow the card to swing behind the hand, by taking the card around with the two fingers which control it. A close-up camera shot (fourth photograph) shows the card at the rear, and the edges of the card (exaggerated here in this picture) gripped between the fingers. The card has vanished. If you wish to finish there your hand comes to the side where your jacket pocket is, and secretly drops the card inside, but if you prefer to produce it again the fifth photograph on p 143 tells the story. Reverse the procedure of the vanish so that the fingers manipulate the card whilst the thumb retains its grip, thus causing the card to appear in view.

VANISHING A STACK OF CARDS

So far we have learnt how to vanish a playing card, but perhaps you would like to vanish almost a complete pack. Difficult? Well, it is easier than the single card vanish already explained. Simple because the method used is a cheeky one, but effective, too.

It is a good climax to a card presentation. About three-quarters of a pack of cards is taken and held in the left

117

hand whilst a fan of cards from the remainder of the pack is made with the right. The first photograph on p 144 shows the positions of the cards at this early stage. The following photograph shows us how the right hand holding the fan comes up in front of the stack of cards being held in the left. This covers the stack completely for a few moments. The next move is rather difficult to explain but behind this fan the stack is clipped with the loose fingers and at the same time the left hand comes up with back outwards as though it were holding the cards. I think the third photograph gives a true picture from the audience's view. The dotted lines on the fan show just where the stack has been left. The right hand 'fans the back of the hand' with a neat flourish. The fourth photograph shows the left hand being opened gradually to show the cards have vanished. At the same time the cards in the right hand are allowed to drop into one stack, or tossed into a hat, thus taking away the evidence of your deception.

Almost any small objects can be vanished by this method. A packet of cigarettes, a soft ball made from sponge, even a flower-head taken from your lapel, can be secretly gripped at the rear of the fan whilst the left hand carries out the operation of supposedly holding the object. Instead of a fan of cards, use a folding fan (as used by the ladies to keep cool).

5

The Big Show

THE FLOWER GIRL ILLUSION

IN THIS chapter of stage magic I am pleased to detail a full-stage illusion. Although the apparatus appears to be large and one would imagine, expensive, the item is in fact within the reach of anyone, even on a small budget.

There are no building plans to follow, only the simple instructions.

This is the type of illusion which can only be presented on a stage or platform. It can be used at small functions such as church concerts, school shows, boy scout evenings etc, and for professional use on the music-hall, at theatres, on television, and so on.

I devised a large version of this item for television some years ago. The method which I am now describing has been simplified but the item is every bit as effective.

EFFECT

The curtains of the stage open to reveal a simple table, set back towards the rear. The performer emphasises there is nothing on the table, even sitting on top of it. A folding screen is now brought on and an assistant places this round the front of the table, hiding it momentarily from view. The magician stands back, takes a pistol, fires. The screen topples over (or it can be removed). A young lady is now sitting on top of the table, and its entire top is covered with bunches and vases of flowers! The girl in a colourful costume wearing a picture bonnet, with a basket of flowers on her arm, represents a flower-seller. A startling effect that can be a good climax to any show.

KNOW-HOW

The method used is an old but reliable one. A four-legged table is used as illustrated. On to the back of the table is pinned a piece of cloth which matches the background to be used. You should use a dark-coloured background. Let us assume that it is black, and a piece of black cloth to match is pinned, with drawing pins, between

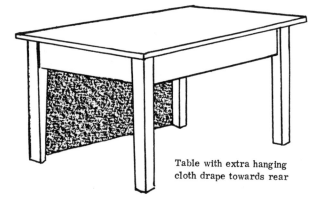

Table with extra hanging
cloth drape towards rear

the legs, at the rear. From a short distance the audience appear to be looking right through the legs of the table and seeing the curtains at the back. If you are working in a small hall it is a good idea to use dark-coloured carpet or a square of black material for the floor. Anything can be concealed behind the legs of the table. In this instance, a girl is there dressed as a flower-seller. With her are several pots of artificial flowers.

PRESENTATION

Performer displays the table, tapping it around with his fist and proving it solid, and really emphasising the fact that it is plain, with nothing on the top. The screen is brought round the front. It is a great help to have someone to assist you here, your own helper, of course. As soon as the screen is in front of the table, the girl behind lifts up the flowers making a quick display on the table. She can, if you wish, remove the black cloth at this stage, from between the legs of the table, pinning this over the top of the table or underneath it. She gets on top of the table, holding a few of the flowers in her hands. The magician stands back, fires the blank gun. Now the girl can reach forward, toppling the screen, or this can be removed. There's the girl amongst the flowers. A pretty effect.

A Variation to this Method is to have the flowers attached to a threefold screen. This screen exactly fills the space between the legs at the rear of the table. The wings which come out at the sides, make the trick more angle-proof and thus more suitable for performance in small halls. These wings on the front of the screen are covered with material to match the back-cloth. On the back of the screen are attached flowers. All the assistant does, when the screen is placed in front, is to lift the screen up and place it on the table. Wings with flowers attached come down at the sides. The girl then gets on to the table-top amongst the flowers.

The masking principle which I've described has a lot of uses in stage magic. You will find the illusion is heightened if the table you use is white or some other light colour,

121

forming a definite outline in contrasted emphasis to the black background. Artificial flowers are easily obtained, and for very little cost you should be able to build quite a pleasant finale to any programme and one which is easily adaptable. For example, in a pageant you could produce Britannia, or the Carnival Queen, and so on.

HAND CREMATION

The next effect is really an illusionette, one that can be easily carried about. When the performer gets an assistant on-stage for use in a daring effect, the audience are always interested in what is going to happen, and this is such an illusion. As the audience sees it, the magician asks for a spectator to come from the audience to help with the trick. When one volunteers, he is asked upon the stage. The performer displays a decorated metal box, showing it to be empty inside and out. That it is empty is quite easy to see and the performer draws attention to a hole which runs from one side to the other, and which is just large enough to take the spectator's arm. The spectator is asked to place his arm right through the hole and into the box, and the front door is dropped down to enable the audience to see it there. Closed up once more, the performer displays pieces of cottonwool and puts these into the top of the box. Striking a match he lights the wool and there is a fantastic flash of fire shooting out of the box.

The front door is now opened and the audience can clearly see that the spectator's arm has completely vanished. To conclude the effect, the door is closed again, and, seconds later, his arm is restored and quite unharmed.

You will agree with me when I say that the above is off the beaten track, and now I would like to describe the apparatus used in this experiment.

The illustration will better explain the making of the metal box. This box should measure 18 in x 12 in x 9 in and has a drop-down door at the front and a hinged door at the top. The complete interior of the box is painted matt black. Two holes, just large enough to take a normal arm, are bored at each end, but not directly in the centre. They should be bored towards one side, as illustrated.

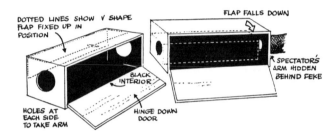

To complete the box, the secret piece is added, and you will see this again illustrated. This piece is hinged on to the back of the inside of the box with a strong black cloth tape. When it is hinged in this position, and when the audience looks inside the box, it looks quite empty and ordinary, but when the 'feke' is allowed to hinge down, it forms a cover within the two holes at each side. This, as you will no doubt guess, is also painted matt black, and finally to keep it up in position during the effect until required, a small strip is stuck on to the inside of the top door. When the door is opened, the strip goes with it and thus lets the 'feke' fall downwards.

Although I advise the entire apparatus be made in metal, there is no reason why wood would not do equally as well. The only reason I mentioned metal was that when working with fire, a metal prop is by far the safer.

Only one other thing is required and that is a supply of

'Flash Wool', the well known material that gives off a flash when lit.

To prepare for the effect, simply have the 'feke' up in position with the top closed and secure it in this position. The front door should also be closed, and your supply of flash wool, together with a box of matches, should be on the table beside the prop. You are all set to begin the experiment.

First, ask for any volunteer from your audience to help you in the experiment, if you may call it such. When you get someone, have him or her seated near the table. Next, lift up the box from the table and open the front door, showing the inside, and as you open the top door, too, have the box slanted towards the back a little so the 'feke' will not fall down. Close the top door, now securing the 'feke', and then the other door. Ask the spectator to push his arm through one side of the box, and out at the other side. Whilst you are doing this, the front door is allowed to drop open so the audience can clearly see his arm is inside the box. Once this has been proved, close the front door. Next, you display the cottonwool and you are now going to place it inside the box, and in so doing, the flap falls down in the correct position, right over the spectator's arm. The flash wool now rests on the metal flap and when it is lit will flare up. Remember to keep the top door open so the audience can see the flashes come out. Now comes the surprise, for when you close the top door and open down the front—THE SPECTATOR'S ARM HAS VANISHED.

Thanks to the black flap against the similar interior, the black art principle shows the vanish to good effect. All that remains is to close the front door again and then ask the spectator to remove his arm.

All is well—the spectator is happy—and the performer gets the applause.

Page 125: Marvellous money box (42) *Revealing slot cut in side of money box. Coin slides out;* (43) *coins placed inside, slide into palm;* (44) *stack of coins concealed in right hand. Coin being peeled off*

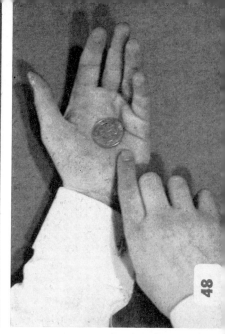

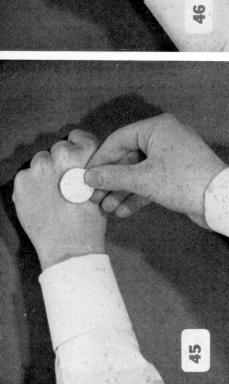

Page 126: Melt through coin (45) Coin displayed in front of the fist; (46) right hand, holding coin, commences to push the fist; (47) right hand, now covers the coin; (48) left hand opens to show coin has now penetrated through

NOVELTY PHOTOGRAPH ILLUSION

Here is another ambitious problem, one with simple properties, which has quite a stunning effect. It is an ideal snappy piece of magic, one that goes over quickly and is ideal for introducing your assistant on stage. Upon the stage, when the curtain opens, is a large novelty photographer's display board (the type which has a cartoon drawing painted on it, with a cut-out space for the head to be inserted) and the performer entering from side stage happens to 'notice' it there. He goes over to the board to have a look. He opens it out showing all sides, then closes the front drape curtain, which has been fixed to a framework. Upon reopening it, the cut-out space is now filled by a girl's head, smiling at the performer. The assistant comes out and is introduced into the act.

I am sure you will agree that here is a fine opening number and you will even be happier when I tell you that it really isn't too difficult to make it up.

So far, I have told you of the actual effect as seen by the audience; now we go backstage and examine the apparatus and working.

First of all you must procure a large piece of hardboard, obtainable from most handicraft shops. This should measure 6 ft x 3 ft and a framework should be nailed around it to make it stronger. Upon this board you have a comedy picture (or pin up) painted to your own specifications. The board is cut out where the head should be. You will also require a framework of the same size, upon which you pin a drape cloth. A wooden strip measuring 6 ft x 6 in is now hinged between those two panels as in the illustration.

Finally, to complete the apparatus, little wheel casters are fitted to the bottom of both panels. You are now all set to rehearse with this item, that is, if you have an assistant ready. You have? Well, let's go!

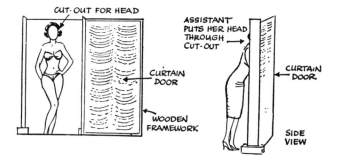

The working is extremely easy. Before the actual performance, have the boards in a V shape in the centre of the floor, with your assistant hiding behind the cut-out panel. She should be crouched down waiting for the performer to start.

The performer draws attention to the boards. He closes the draped front, the assistant still being behind the cut-out panel. He now opens the front, and assistant immediately crawls from behind cut-out one and goes behind the drape.

The cut-out panel is now hinged to the front showing the other side, and then swung back. The assistant goes back to her original position whilst the performer closes the front once more. When closed she pops her head through the cut out.

The magician fires a blank cartridge gun towards the boards and quickly opens the front to show the production of the girl in this novel manner.

The assistant then comes out and to the front to take a bow. As you will see, the apparatus should fold completely flat and you will find that it will cost very little to make.

I do hope you will give it a try, for it's quite novel.

A STARTLING SACK ESCAPE

The famous escapologist, Harry Houdini, boasted that no chains could hold him.

Here's a stunning escape that I've used myself to good effect, but which is very simple indeed to perform.

Magician draws attention to a large sack made from sateen or some lightweight material. The bag is thoroughly examined. The magician steps into the sack, the top of which is tightly tied. A screen is placed round him. Immediately the magician shouts, 'One, two, three!' and as quickly as *that* he steps from behind the screen with the sack over his arm! The knots are all still intact!

HERE'S HOW

The method is cheeky, and simplicity itself. The sack is made from material and sewn on the sides only; the bottom is left open! Pieces of material are turned in and hemmed independently. To keep these together a thread is passed through as illustrated; one end of thread terminates in a large knot, while the other hangs loose. After the sack has been examined (and you will find that it *can* be examined, for it appears perfectly ordinary) the magician has only to take hold of the knot and pull the thread out to leave him with a mere tube of material. It is not necessary to do this yourself. You can have an assistant go round with the sack, passing it to be examined, and he or she pulls the thread out on the way back to the stage. Or you can have a stooge (someone who helps you with the working of the trick) who pulls the thread out during the examination of the bag. The rest is really all showmanship.

Get into the sack, making sure that you do not reveal the true nature of things. Turn the bottom inwards and stand

129

on it to prevent the deception from being seen. Now have

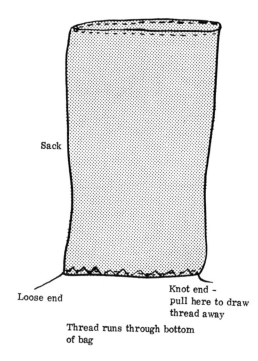

Sack

Loose end

Knot end –
pull here to draw
thread away

Thread runs through bottom
of bag

the top tied, etc, with a great deal of fuss and showmanship. The moment that the screen is placed round, you have
only to pull the sack up over your head to effect the escape!

If you wish you can play the part of the master-illusion-
ist, placing your girl assistant inside the sack. The screen is
placed around, you walk behind the screen, and straight
away the girl assistant marches out.

Of course, the moment the screen is placed around she
gets out of the sack, and leaves this on the floor ready for
you to just slip over your head. Straight away she removes
the screen, revealing that you are in the sack, and then

130

cuts through the knots at the top of the sack to release you
—a quick substitution.

You will find the apparatus for this item very cheap and
easy to make. Remember, the real secret of magic is the
showmanship in putting it over.

A SPECTACULAR SACK ILLUSION

Here's an illusion that embodies a clever escape principle.
It has been specially designed for this book of magic.

The magician introduces his girl assistant. A cloth bag
is passed to a committee from the audience to examine
thoroughly. The girl steps into the bag, the top is pulled
up, and members of the committee now tie the top of the
bag tightly with ropes. The magician displays a screen, which
has a hole in the front of it, and places it round the sack.
He pulls the top of the sack, which is visible to the audience,
right through the hole so that it is hanging in front.
Obviously escape of any kind is quite impossible for the
young lady.

Spectators hold the ropes which come from the sack, and
on the count of three they are to pull. After a few false
starts and a bit of byplay, the count of three is given. The
spectators pull and the sack passes right through the hole.
The spectators check that the knots are still intact. The rope
is quickly cut off the top. The magician reaches inside the
sack and produces from it—the young lady's dress! There
is a bit of comedy byplay. Will the magician remove the
screen? Finally he does so. The young lady is there but,
she is holding a towel in front of her!

Alternatively, on the count of three when the spectators
pull, the young lady can scream and dash from behind the
screen in her undies, running off to the side of the stage.
The magician now cuts the ropes and from the sack re-

131

moves the young lady's dress, tossing it to the side where she is.

HERE'S HOW

The method is very, very simple. Two lightweight sacks are used. These are made from black sateen or similar lining materials. The assistant has one of the sacks under her dress at the start, and this sack already contains a lightweight dress similar to that which she is wearing. After the first sack has been examined, the young lady steps inside it. When she is inside the sack, she reaches under her dress, pulling down the duplicate sack. When the magician closes the top of the sack over, bunching this around, the young

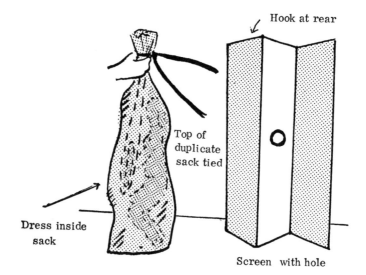

Hook at rear

Top of
duplicate
sack tied

Dress inside
sack

Screen with hole

lady inside pushes up the neck of the duplicate sack. The magician places his hands round the sacks to hide any junction. About nine inches or so of the inner sack is allowed to protrude, and it is this portion of sack which is tied by the spectators. All the time the magician retains his grip on the sack. Now when the screen is placed around, it is this tied top that is pulled through. Behind the screen the young lady steps out of the outer sack, slips out of her dress, places the latter in the sack and hangs this on a hook behind the screen. She is ready to scream at the appropriate moment and dash off-stage.

Alternatively, she has a towel also under her dress at the start and now merely holds this in front to partially 'hide her blushes'!

The cost of making this illusion is almost nil, yet its entertainment value will be found to be very considerable.

The principle of the double sack is quite a clever one, and you can make the same thing up in miniature and performing a baffling effect with a gold watch, which can apparently pass right through the sack, and so on. A little thought with this trick, as with others in magic, will reveal endless possibilities.

6

Magic of the Mind

THERE is no such thing as mindreading, or controlled telepathy, at least in my opinion. The stage or television mentalist certainly relies on trickery to bring about his effects.

It is truly amazing the number of people who, in fact, do believe in mindreading, and misguidedly imagine that the entertainer who is earning £30 (approx $75) a week can actually read people's minds, predict the results of football coupons, and do so many unlikely things. If he could *indeed* do these things, he would surely be so busy filling in the football coupons, predicting things which are to happen, weeks before, and earning so much money that his little world of entertainment would not even be a sideline.

Mindreading depends on trickery. I will go one step further and say it consists of ten per cent trickery, and ninety per cent *showmanship,* for without this latter ingredient you could not successfully present to your audience your experiments as mental mysteries, or experiments in extrasensory perception. One has to play the part of a genuine mindreader under stress and strain, exactly as though he was reading someone's mind. The days of working fast with mindreading experiments have gone, and it is the normal practice to present the programme quietly and slowly, building up to and dramatising the climax to leave the audience with an impression of your powers as a telepathist and to reap the applause.

Already in the book I have given a few near mental and mindreading effects, but the ones detailed here use no bulky apparatus, for a mindreader doesn't really require apparatus to read someone's mind, or predict something which is going to happen. Neverthless, we use pieces of paper, pencils, envelopes, etc—items which are natural, but not brightly coloured. I am not suggesting that colour must never play a part in this type of entertainment, far from it. 'Colour Jars', an item which appears in this chapter, is entirely based on colour, and the performer can name the sequence of colours which the spectator has freely selected. The same applies to the 'Crayon and Tube Mystery', also described, colour again being the basis of the effect. But the natural props should not be gaudy, but ordinary and natural looking.

Before starting a mindreading programme, study the following points.

1. Use normal properties: for example, a polished table rather than a brightly coloured one.

2. Try to avoid mixing these experiments with normal magical tricks. If this is done, the audience in the end will think that everything you have done was just another trick.

3. If any item should misfire, through your carelessness or through no fault of yours, remember you call these 'experiments' and experiments *can* go wrong. A trick must never go wrong, but on many occasions 'mindreaders' deliberately make mistakes to make it look as though it is the real thing.

PAPER THOUGHT

The first item uses a piece of paper and a pen, and most important of all, the assistance of a member of the audience.

The performer makes it clear that the spectator he has chosen is not working in collusion with him, and that he uses no 'stooges' during the entire show.

A small square of paper is handed to the spectator and he is asked to write down any question right in the centre of the mystic circle which is boldly marked upon it. This the spectator does. He is then told to fold the paper in half, with the writing inside, and then again in quarters, thus concealing the information.

The performer reaches out for the paper, then tears it into pieces, which he then burns over an ashtray until nothing but ashes remain. The performer slowly 'gets the impression' of the spectator's question, and actually starts to answer it! To the audience it is unbelievable. How could he know what the spectator was thinking about!

KNOW-HOW

In magical circles the simple move which is employed for the presentation of this experiment is called 'the centre tear', and I will explain exactly what this means and what happens.

Have a square of paper about 4 in square. In the centre of the paper boldly draw a circle with the aid of a pair of compasses or a round object. Have the paper upon your table together with a pen or pencil. An ashtray and box of matches are also required. In performance a spectator is asked to assist by taking the square paper and pen, and to think of a question which he would like to have answered: something in his mind, which no one knows at this present

moment; a question concerning love, finance, etc. When he
has thought of such a question, the performer asks him to

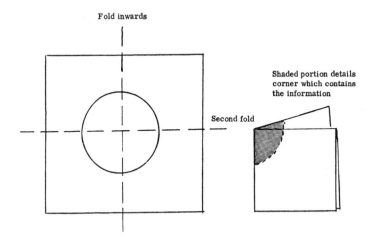

Fold inwards

Shaded portion details
corner which contains
the information

Second fold

write this boldly on the paper to 'isolate his thought'. Of
course, the spectator has to write in the central position, but
the performer doesn't have to mention this aloud; he merely
points to the inside of the circle as he hands the paper to the
man, requesting him to write his question down. The performer moves well back from the spectator during the writing, where it is impossible for him to see this being done. The
spectator is now requested to fold the paper in half, with the
question facing inwards, and then again, so it is now a neat
folded slip. The performer takes the folded paper from the
spectator. He holds it between his right thumb and forefinger, firmly gripping it. The paper is held at the folded-over
portion so that the writing comes under the thumb. Now
the paper is torn into pieces. First it is torn down and then
across, but the piece of paper with the writing is still kept
under the thumb.

137

Transfer all the torn pieces except the concealed one to the left hand. Now, take a matchbox from the right-hand jacket pocket and at the same time leave the 'stolen' piece of paper behind in the pocket. Strike a match, setting fire to the pieces on view and allowing them to fall into the ashtray. It is a good idea to have a little spirit in the ashtray, the flames adding to the effect. Move right away from the burning paper, replacing the matchbox in your pocket and at the same time taking out the small piece of paper again, opening this out and keeping it concealed in the fingers. As you move away from the burning paper and spectator, you will find it an easy matter to glance down at the question.

Place both hands to the forehead if you have any difficulty at all, bringing the slip up before the eyes. It is then up to you to answer the question in as dramatic a manner as possible.

Of course the answer might not be correct, but, as with fortune telling, a favourable answer can do no harm.

For example, if the spectator asks, 'Will I get married soon?' the performer, who during the routine is not supposed to know what the question is about, states, 'I can see in your mind you are thinking ahead. I believe you are looking forward to perhaps . . . a happy event. A woman is in your life or may come into your life very soon, but . . . wait . . . things are rather blurred at this moment, and time can play tricks on us all. I know you are going to be extremely happy when the event comes along'.

In several short statements you have gradually told the spectator what he wants to hear yet you have not told a lie. Furthermore you give the impression that all of the things you mention have been the thoughts of the spectator. The same applies with any question, whether it be 'Shall I travel soon?' or 'Will I win the football pools?' etc. Another presentation using this same 'centre tear' is to have the spectator make a design upon the paper, right in the central position. You can have a large card or blackboard on which are drawn quite a number of designs such as a circle, square, triangle etc, and when you retain the centre piece you have the design right in the palm of your hand. Now you can duplicate the design on the back of the board, or 'ring around' the design which has been selected on the front, after suitable hesitancy and showmanship, of course.

DEAD AND ALIVE MATCHBOXES

With a few matchboxes, slips of paper, and a paper bag, you are set to present a really stunning little mental experiment which is extremely easy to do.

The great thing about this one particular item is that no preparation is required before or after the show, and this means it is always ready to perform.

In effect, five matchboxes are used and five members of the audience each receive one, together with a slip of paper and a pencil. Four spectators are asked to assist by writing down the name of a living person, preferably a personality whom everyone knows. The fifth spectator is asked to write down the name of a dead person, again, preferably, a well known figure who has passed away.

They are asked to fold their papers and place them inside their matchbox, closing the tray. A paper bag is next shown and the spectators are asked to hand over their boxes. One at a time they are dropped inside the bag, and the entire lot are shaken around, thus making it even more difficult for the performer to know which one contains the dead name. Suddenly the performer reaches inside the bag and removes a matchbox but remarks, 'This contains a live name'. Another, then one more, until the fourth box is removed and he stops. 'I get the impression that this box contains the dead name,' says the performer. Handing it over to a member of the audience to open, he is found to be correct.

KNOW-HOW

The secret is simple, so simple one would hardly wonder whether it would baffle any audience . . . *but it does!*

As described above, five matchboxes are required and these are unfeked. Five slips of paper, five pencils, and a paper bag, are your other requirements, all of them being perfectly genuine. The secret is not in the apparatus but

Matchbox opened as
it is placed inside
the bag

in the cheeky move which takes place when the matchboxes are being placed inside the bag one at a time. When all the paper slips have been written upon, and then folded and firmly placed inside the boxes by the spectators themselves, come forward and collect the boxes. These are held in a batch and placed upon the table, but you must remember the position of the box which contains the dead name. The mouth of the brown paper bag is opened, and the first box is shown and dropped inside, then the second, both of which contains 'live names'. When you drop in the 'dead name', your thumb pushes up the tray of the box so that it is really *slightly opened*. This is done, of course, under cover as you are actually placing it deep inside the bag. The other two are placed in but just like the first two, unopened. All the shaking in the world, will not close the opened box, yet it is an easy matter for you to find the 'dead' name immediately.

Of course, it would be unwise for you to pull this one out first. Give your audience a little suspense by first bringing out two or perhaps three of the others, and then come to the one which you suddenly react to. At this point you act a little as though something tells you, 'This is the dead name'. When you bring this one out you close the tray of the box and it looks exactly like the previous ones. Never leave this box until the last, for I have found it is better to find it between the others. The wonderful part of the effect is that everything can be thoroughly examined, for there is nothing for the audience to find. A real mystery with a simple, simple method.

SO SIMPLE CARD PREDICTION

This is one of the simplest methods of predicting a certain card that has ever been used. It is unbelievable that the average person doesn't know exactly what lies within an ordinary die (dice).

The performer borrows a pack of cards, riffles through it for a second and then names one of the cards. He chalks its name upon a slate, and then hands a spectator two dice. The spectator is requested to throw the dice upon the table and then to add the two top numbers together, turn the dice over and add on the two bottom numbers which have been thrown. The addition totals 14, and the spectator is asked to count down to the fourteenth card, reverse it, and compare it with the chalked prediction on the slate. True enough, the performer's prediction is correct!

KNOW-HOW

You will have noticed that I said 'the addition totals 14' and this is *always* the number, no matter how the dice are thrown. Try for yourself, the top numbers plus the bottom always add to 14. At the commencement of the trick, in front of the audience, you fan through the pack, remembering the fourteenth card from the top, and it is the name of this card which you write upon the slate. The rest of the experiment works itself!

COLOUR JARS

Some years ago a popular trick with magicians was one with rings, balls, or cubes, each of a different colour. They were placed by a spectator into a box, the order of the colours being secretly noted. The magician would reveal the colour combination, and he was always correct.

We take this old trick, throw away the usual props, and, instead, use clear jars. Furthermore, we have added a new climax to give the experiment the perfect ending.

Six small glass jars are shown, each with a different coloured screw-on lid. Red, yellow, green, blue, white, and black, are the colours I myself use. The jars are of the type that have a shoulder so the screw-on top is of smaller diameter than the jars. A long narrow box, complete with a lid (as illustrated, to help you obtain or make one), is used to hold the jars in one line with the lids uppermost. The audience can clearly see each cap is of a different colour,

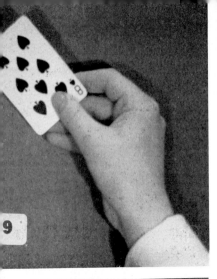

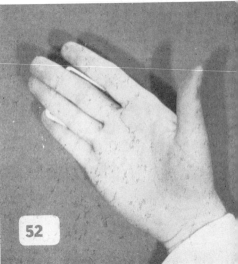

age 143: Vanishing and producing a card
*9) Position of holding playing card prior
* its vanish; (50) note card being pushed
*p slightly; (51) index finger and little finger
*url over edges of card; (52) fingers pivot
*ackwards, taking card out of view. Note
*xaggerated edges of card; (53) reverse pro-
cedure, bringing card back into view

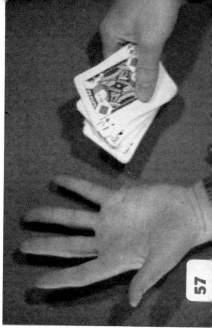

Page 144: Vanishing a stack of cards (54) *Left hand holds stack of cards whilst right displays a fan in front; (55) fan of cards cover the stack completely; (56) dotted lines show the stack of cards being retained behind the fan whilst left hand carries upwards as though holding them; (57) the final 'vanish'. Left hand fingers open slowly*

and, of course, when the jars are moved around, it is possible to have many colour combinations.

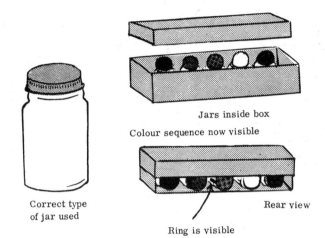

Jars inside box
Colour sequence now visible

Correct type
of jar used

Rear view

Ring is visible

The performer turns aside whilst he explains to a spectator just what he would like him or her to do. He asks the spectator to borrow a ring or coin from another member of the audience and to place it inside any one of the jars, and to note the jar with this particular colour on top. This has to be placed along with the others, and the colours should be facing the top of the open box. The spectator may then move the jars around, rearranging them in any sequence. When this has been done, the spectator is further requested to place the lid on the box, thus hiding the jars from view. The performer then asks that the closed box should be placed into his own hands, held behind his back.

He then turns to face the spectators.

With the box held behind his back he does one simple 'move', and it is that of removing the lid, tilting over the

145

body of the box so it is now on its side, and then replacing the lid back on top. As our illustration shows, the lid
really goes over what originally was the side of the box, and
so half of the coloured tops are now visible from the back
—enough to reveal the colours.

As the performer recaps on what has happened so far, he
brings the box to the front, and a mere glance enables him
to obtain the information he requires. He can reveal the
sequence of colours one by one, and the ring or coin which
has been placed inside one particular jar can be seen lying
flat on the side of the upturned jar (thanks to the fact that
the jars have a neck slightly smaller than the body of the
jar). After stating the colour sequence he reveals that the
ring was placed inside, say, the red-topped jar. Immediately
the spectator confirms that the mentalist's assertions are
correct, the performer takes his applause, and then quickly
takes off the lid to prove that everything is as it should be.
In doing this, he removes the lid with the left hand, whilst
the right pivots over the box, thus showing the coloured tops
in the top position. Practise making this turnover move
slickly and without hesitation.

Don't forget to return the borrowed ring or coin! It's
easy to overlook doing so during the applause which comes.

CRAYON AND TUBE MYSTERY

Again, colour is the keynote here.

Six coloured crayons and a metal corked tube are the
requirements for this effect.

Whilst the 'mindreader' turns his back to the audience
a spectator assists by placing a chosen coloured crayon
into the thin tube, finally securing the cork or screw-cap
in position. The tube is handed to the performer who almost
immediately reveals the chosen colour.

KNOW-HOW

Like the previous effect, a secret move enables you to reveal the correct colour, for the items used are unprepared. Obtain six crayons of different colours, and a metal capsule of the type that is normally filled with pills, etc. Whether it has a cork stopper or a screw-on cap doesn't really matter, as long as the tube can be firmly secured. Your local chemist or drug store should be able to provide you with a suitable container.

The spectator who assists in this experiment selects a colour freely, and places it inside the tube, sealing it with the stopper. This is done whilst the performer turns away from the audience. All the other crayons are pocketed by the spectator, then the tube containing the single crayon is handed to the performer, who stands with both his hands held behind his back.

Coloured mark made on thumb-nail

The performer then turns and faces the audience. It is the secret 'doings' which go on behind his back that make the trick possible. The performer removes the stopper quickly, and rubs the crayon against the thumb-nail to place a coloured mark on it. The stopper is replaced in position, and, for a moment, the performer's right hand comes to the front and to his brow as though he were really concentrating deeply. Of course, what happens is that as his right hand comes towards the brow, the performer quickly glances at the coloured mark on his thumb. He sees the colour, and can now pretend to divine the spectator's thoughts. The tube, still containing the crayon, can immediately be handed to the spectator, for it is still intact and there is no trickery to be found.

Easy as it may be to perform this experiment, the effect does register with any audience, and the entire procedure may be repeated again for a second showing—but no further. Remember where to stop, for the performer who gets carried away with himself may be very disappointed in the end!

SEALED PREDICTION

Our final 'test' is a prediction—one which seems hard to believe.

The performer displays a piece of paper upon which he makes a prediction. It is placed inside an envelope which is sealed.

A pack of borrowed cards is used and it is cut by a spectator. To mark the position of the 'cut' the envelope is placed between the two halves, so that nothing can be altered. Another spectator is asked to remove the top half of the pack, take away the envelope and open it and read out the prediction. Inside, written upon this slip of paper is, 'The spectator will cut the cards at the four of diamonds'. When the spectator is asked to lift the top card of the bottom half of the pack, it is found to be the very card which the performer has predicted.

KNOW HOW

As I have already mentioned, the cards may be borrowed, which adds considerably to the effect. The vital thing the performer must do is to remember the top card, and this can be easily done as the cards are fanned for display prior to the prediction being made. It is the name of this card which is written before the audience on the slip of paper which is sealed inside the envelope. The envelope containing this prediction is rested on top of the pack for a few moments as the performer recaps on what has been done so far. When the envelope is again lifted away the top card is also secretly taken away, and you will find there is plenty of cover here, thanks to the size of the envelope.

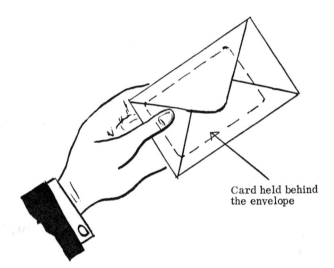

Card held behind
the envelope

A spectator is asked to cut the cards at any part of the pack, and this is where the envelope is inserted together with the hidden card, which has thus been secretly added to the top of the bottom half of the pack. All that remains is for the spectator to remove the top half of the pack, lift up the envelope, open it and read out the prediction, and then for you, finally, to display the 'cut-at card' as being the one that you had predicted before the experiment began! Easy? I told you it was, which means that you can devote most of the work to the *presentation* and make a simple trick into a real 'mindreading miracle'.

CONCLUSION

I HOPE you have enjoyed my book on magic, but more than that, I hope it will have shown you the way to become a successful conjurer.

A book of magic is not like a novel, it is a book to be *referred to*. I hope that this one will be for you the start of an enjoyable hobby for life.

Whether the fruits of your labour should be used to enable you to earn a living as a professional, or merely as a pleasing diversion, is for you, the individual, to decide. I started my own magical career many years ago when I received a small box of conjuring tricks as a birthday present. Pursuing my hobby further, my services were in demand at charity concerts, and although I did not make any money from these functions they did provide me with the experience I needed. From there, other types of bookings came along—some big, some small, but all rewarding. Children's parties, cabaret spots, and, finally, television shows. At this point in my life I had one ambition, and that was to be in magic *really* full time, and so I forsook the limelight in order to turn my energies to the more inventive side of our art.

A tremendous amount of material that started off as 'just a thought' has ended up in the programmes of top-line magicians. It sounds very much like a 'local boy makes good' story, doesn't it? But it is true.

What is the secret of success? Is it capital? Knowing the right people? A gift? No, dear reader, it is none of these things and I, certainly, had none of them. The real secret is in one simple word, and that is ENTHUSIASM. Yes, it works. Try it!

BIBLIOGRAPHY

Recommended Magic Reading

HOW many books on magic have been published over the years no one can guess. Though the number is quite unbelievable, running into many thousands, the majority of these books have been published for magicians only and contain strictly advanced magic. These books were written for the reader who was already familiar with the principles of the art. On many occasions, different moves, sleight-of-hand methods, etc, are referred to by name only, as it is assumed that the reader already knows what this particular part of the trick is about. These are professional books, written for the professional or semi-professional magical entertainer.

Magic books fall into many different categories. Name almost any articles—rope, dice, candles, balls, etc—and a book of magic has been devoted to tricks using them. Several encyclopaedias cover all the principles and methods of that particular branch of magic among the contents.

Producing such books is not such a rewarding proposition, for the publishers usually have a very limited sale, because of the very specialised nature of the subject tackled. That is why such books are often expensive to buy, but each has something that can further the art of magic, and without magical publishers our art would be a dying one.

It would be impossible to detail every book that has been published dealing with magic, for it would have to contain thousands of pages; so I intend to give the reader a list of good magical books covering almost every branch of the art.

CARD MANIPULATIONS
Television Card Manipulations, by Ian Adair (The Supreme

Magic Publishing Company, Devon), is not a large book, but one which covers the entire basic moves of producing cards singly or in fans. Photographs give the reader a good view of the productions, but in most cases patience and practice are required for the presentation of these manipulations.

CIGARETTES

Encyclopaedia of Cigarette Tricks, by Keith Clark (Tannen Publications, USA)

The author of this fine publication was a touring professional, making his money from his branch of the profession—magic with cigarettes. The countless methods, the many gadgets used, are unbelievable, and are described here with the aid of photographs and line drawings. It took the author some thirty years to compile and write the volume.

CUPS AND BALLS

The reader will now be familiar with the classic 'Cups and Balls' trick, for our own routine using a gardening theme, has been explained in this book (p 105). This is one of the oldest and most talked about tricks ever to be released to the fraternity, and the following book covers many exciting and different slants to this great trick.

The Last Word on Cups and Balls, by Eddie Joseph (The Supreme Magic Publishing Company, Devon)

In this 70-page illustrated book, Eddie Joseph of Bombay (the author of many fine books on magic), includes many moves and originalities which can be introduced into the sequence of manipulations using three cups and three balls. Some of his ideas include liquid being produced within the cups, or a live canary, and his detailed methods are explained in simple language.

153

BIBLIOGRAPHY: RECOMMENDED MAGIC READING

DOVES

The Encyclopaedia of Dove Magic, by Ian Adair (The Supreme Magic Publishing Company, Devon)

In this modern age of magic and bewilderment, a magician is not a magician unless he produces some doves in his act. This is why the author has studied worldwide methods for years, carefully detailing them, illustrating them with drawings and photographs, and releasing them to the brotherhood of magic. Here in this one work, containing several hundred pages, the student is taught step by step how to produce, vanish, and change the colour of doves under any conditions. This book is a highly specialised one, as, too, is *Television Dove Magic* in which many of the star names in Magic contribute the favourite tricks and routines that have won each acclaim over the years.

FOR THE BEGINNER

The Puffin Book of Magic, by Norman Hunter (Penguin Books)

Strictly for the beginner who is interested in magic. South African born Norman Hunter provides his readers (and these include children), with many novel and entertaining puzzles and tricks in his 128-page paperback. The book is well illustrated and the items used are mainly normal household commodities.

GENERAL MAGIC

Opus Thirteen, by Eric C. Lewis (Goodliffe Publications, Birmingham)

Author of many good magical books for magicians, Eric Lewis made it a point to build each piece of apparatus and present it many times before an audience, before he described it in print. By doing this he made sure he could overcome the snags which so often happen during the construction and performance of a new piece of apparatus. All the items in his book have been tried and tested and are appealing to any audience. Highly recommended for the magician who is seeking clever and original magical miracles.

Simply Wizard, by Goodliffe. (Goodliffe Publications)
The author, editor of the famous magical magazine, *Abracadabra,* gathered together many fine magical items for his readers here, and the highlight of his book is his version of the 'Leg Chopper', an illusion which has stood the test of time. A girl's leg, placed through a 'stock' is chopped off and restored. The full plans, measurements, and details are illustrated with line drawings and photographs in this fine publication.

Tarbell Course in Magic, by Harlan Tarbell (Tannen Publications, USA)
The finest complete course in magic ever published for the student of the art. Dr Harlan Tarbel! spent many years compiling this American work, which covers every branch of magic from coin magic to stage illusions. Each volume containing about 500 pages, the six volumes in all contain thousands of tricks, clearly described and with excellent line drawings by Tarbell himself. The *Tarbell Course* is often referred to as the Magicians' Bible. These volumes are expensive, but expense is no object when acquiring the correct information, properly detailed and nicely produced.

MECHANICAL MAGIC
The Magic of Louis Histed, by Louis Histed. (Goodliffe Publications, Birmingham)

Undoubtedly one of the greatest magical inventors of our time, the late Louis Histed will be remembered for the many great principles which he gave the art. These were, indeed, scientific miracles beyond his time, and the book which he has left behind him will honour his memory for ever.

In this 160-page bound book, he details mechanical tricks with extremely clever principles, and yet every one is practical, for he demonstrated them over the years at those magical conventions that he attended as the star guest lecturer. Many items described are difficult to build, unless one is skilled at working in various materials, but all *can* be produced. The resulting magical effects are masterpieces, which will baffle audiences for years to come.

PRESENTATION ON STAGE

Showmanship and Presentation, by Edward Maurice (The Supreme Magic Publishing Company, Devon)

Not containing tricks or magical ideas, this book (first published over twenty years ago, and reprinted several times) was written by a magician who made it his concern to improve presentation and add showmanship to each trick, no matter how large or small. The book explains how to 'walk on and off' the stage correctly, how to handle spectators from the audience, how to handle objects smoothly and professionally. This is a book which will teach you professionalism and help you to become a good artiste. Highly recommended to every student of magic.

SILKS

Rice's Encyclopaedia of Silk Magic, by Harold Rice (Silk King Studios, USA)

The author of this three-volume American encyclopaedia has devoted his life to detailing magic with silk handkerchiefs. Each volume of some 500 pages brings the reader many thousands of silk tricks, some simple, some which require great skill. Mechanical apparatus methods are described as well as sleights and moves that must be practised, and the entire set of books deals with the subject admirably.

SPOOKY MAGIC

Daemons, Darklings and Doppelgangers, by Tony Sheils (The Supreme Magic Publishing Company, Devon)

Tony Sheils presents thrilling macabre magic with a whiff of the supernatural. Tony is well known for this brand of sorcery both in Britain and the USA. After his popular *13!!!* book, came *Something Strange,* and now to complete this trilogy of humour comes this latest manual of weird and mysterious effects. Between the spookily designed jacket of green and black depicting odd creatures of the night, he offers magic which is filled with fright. Certainly not the type of entertainment to present at the vicar's tea party or at a children's show, but great stuff for home use.

MAGICAL MAGAZINES

It may not be known to you that a number of magazines, published for magicians, are released periodically. These are not seen on the normal bookstall or newsagent's counter. These are published for the magician and contain new ideas, magical information, different routines on old tricks, new items of interest to magicians, and advertisements of new tricks, illusions, books for the fraternity.

Abracadabra. Weekly. Editor, Goodliffe (Goodliffe Publications, Birmingham)

Each week, this 20-page magazine gets into the hands of many enthusiastic magicians. A well established though limited publication, it covers every branch of the art and offers the student new ideas at a low cost.

The Magigram. Bi-monthly. Editor, Ken de Courcy (The Supreme Magic Publishing Company, Devon)

This 64-page magazine, containing some twenty new tricks fully described in each issue, is published every two months (six issues per year). Star contributors release their pet tricks to the readers, and, as well as news items, advertisements of latest publications, competitions, and previews of magical events, are released. Every student can benefit from this magazine of magic.

The New Pentagram. Monthly. Editor, Peter Warlock. (The Supreme Magic Publishing Company, Devon)

Peter Warlock, author. writer, performer, lecturer, is known to all magicians in every country in this wide world. His name spells MAGIC. His *Pentagram*, an established magazine which contained subtle and sophisticated magic made an immediate hit. Now in new format and style, the *New Pentagram* is packed with brilliant magic. Mr Warlock collects the magic plans from magic's 'greats' and the *New Pentagram* is filled with their tried and tested material. A British publication which has a tremendous overseas (especially USA) following.

AMERICAN MAGAZINES

The Genii. Monthly. Editor, W. Larsen Jnr (Genii Publications, USA)

Direct from Hollywood USA, this magazine of magic is well established in its field, beautifully produced, and includes a versatile range of magical items fully explained. It is slanted towards American magic, but the items are easily adaptable to performance in any country.

The Tops. Monthly. Editor, Niel Foster (Abbott's Manufacturing Company, USA)

This superb magazine of magic uses a number of experienced magicians who each have their own columns within each issue. The contents include reports, experiences in magic, gossip, plus new magical effects described by regular contributors who, over the years, have gone from strength to strength. Every collector of magical literature should make sure he receives this fine magazine of magic.

Of course, there are many other magical magazines, strictly for private circulation—for members of certain societies or clubs—which I cannot detail here. But those I have listed should interest the reader of this book, and enable him to pursue our lively art further still.

159

INDEX OF TRICKS

Italic numbers refer to pages of plates